はじめに

本書、『「私」を語れば、英語は話せる。』の対象とする読者は、

* **英語を楽しく勉強したい方、**
* **英語で日記を書きたい方、**
* **海外移住を夢みる方、**
* **母国語のように英語を話したい方、**
* **英文法が苦手な方、**
* **英語の勉強に何度も挫折している方、**
* **英語は早すぎて聞き取れないという方**など、

英語学習初心者から、さまざまなレベルの方としています。本書の英語学習手法は、どのようなレベルの方にでも活用いただける、とても有効なものです。

本書で継続的にトレーニングすることによって、あなたのスピーキング力とリスニング力がぐんぐん伸びていくことをお約束します。

自分のことを話すのがなぜいいのか？

本書の一番の特長として、語学学習の手法にさまざまなシーンで「自分のことを語る」ことを用いています。これにより、

❶勉強としてではなく、**自らの体験として英語を学べる**
❷自分を語るのであれば、**一人でも進められる**（英会話は一人では学習できないとされている）
❸自分を表現することで、**状況や気持ち、考え、行動**

などを、英語で表現する力が身につく（自分が置かれている状況や、実際の自分の経験に置き換えて話せば、英語力が飛躍的にアップする）

上記3つの効果が期待できるのです。

わたしたちが24時間で思いつく感情や考えは、膨大な語彙数になります。自分にとって最も身近な「言葉」を英語に変換するのですから、自己表現力がどんどん高まります。

「つぶやく」ことの効用

本書の2つ目の特徴は、音声に続けて英語を繰り返す「つぶやき」という手法をとっていることです。

この方式は**赤ちゃんが母国語を周囲の人から自然と学び、獲得していく模倣形式の学習法**です。この方法ならだれでも1年以内に話す力を身につけることができるのです。また何と言っても、「つぶやき」の利点は、お金をかけずにいつでもどこでも練習ができることです。つまり、英会話の学校に行く必要もなく、通勤（通学）途中や帰宅途中に、入浴中に、就寝時に、いつでもどこでも「つぶやく」ことによって英会話の練習をすることができるのです。多忙な毎日を過ごす人にとって、これ以上の学習法はありません。

倍速音声の効果

3つ目の特長は、ノーマルスピードと2倍速スピードの音声をダウンロードできる点です。2倍速スピードによって、**「インターチェンジ効果」**が得られます。高速道路のインターチェンジから一般道路に降りると、実際のスピードよりも遅く感じられます。これは聴覚にも当てはまります。**速いスピードの音声を聴いていると、普通の速さの音声がゆっくりと感じられ、理解が容易になる**のです。速聴を繰り返すことで、**記憶力や集中力をアップさせながら頭の回転を良くし、様々な潜在能力が高められる**ことも、すでに脳科学の分野で立証されています。

これら3つの方法を総合的に使って学習できるのが、本書になります。

私が高校生の頃、英語の勉強方法の中にユニークなものがありました。それは、「目に映るものの中で、これはおもしろそうだと思ったモノを英語で言ってみる」、つまり「つぶやき」です。

例えば、通学途中にトンボが飛んでいれば「トンボは英語で何だっけ？ そう、dragonfly（ドラゴンフライ）だ」と実際につぶやいたものです。その後、「じゃあ、カブトムシは？」「蛍は？」などと、あれこれ思いを巡

らしました。語彙数がかなり増えると、今度は文章でつぶやく練習です。「あっ、あれはカブトムシだ！(Oh, that's a beetle!)」程度の英文から始め、「カブトムシが木に止まってる（There's a beetle on the tree.）」などとつぶやいたものです。

多忙な日々を送る現代人は、自宅でゆっくりと時間を取って勉強をするのは難しいもの。つまり、今も昔も簡単かつ最強の英語勉強法は、本書で紹介する、「私を語るつぶやき勉強法」であることに変わりはありません。

学習方法

❶ **音声をダウンロード**
❷ **テキストは見ずに2倍速スピードで音声を聴く**
❸ **ノーマルスピードで音声を聴く**
❹ **テキストは見ずに音声だけで内容を把握する**
❺ **日本語訳と照らし合わせて確認する**
❻ **英文を見ながらノーマルスピードに合わせて英語をつぶやく**

まずは、音声をダウンロードしていただき（6ページ参照）2倍速スピードを聴きます（どのシーンから学習しても構いません）。**テキストを見ずに音声から聴き始めることがポイント**です。自分のリスニング力を再確認しましょう。徐々に耳が鍛えられていくことを実感できるでしょう。

次にノーマルスピードの音声に切り替えます。2倍速スピードと比べると、音声がゆっくりと感じられるでしょう。ここで**内容をどれくらい理解できるか確認し**てください。

日本語訳は、内容を自分の力で把握してから見るようにします。

シーンを正確に理解できたら、英文を見ながらつぶやきます。1シーンを暗記できるまで繰り返しつぶやきましょう。1週間くらいで暗記できるようにするのが目安です。音声に遅れないように続けて読み上げるようにしてください。

抑揚やイントネーションを真似た**自分の声を聴くことで、リスニング力と発声速度が上がります。**

🔊 音声ダウンロード方法

スマートフォンやパソコンなどで、
本書の音声を無料でダウンロードできます。
下記 URL を直接入力するか、
QR コードを読み取って、
リンク先からダウンロードしてください。

↓

http://www.horei.com/dl/8628032/

1.

ダウンロードした音声のトラックナンバーが記載されています。はじめから順番に学習する必要はありません。関心のあるテーマからはじめてください。

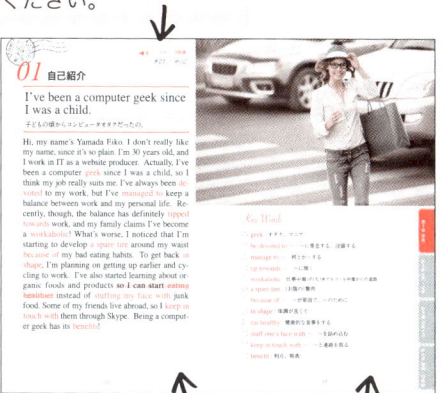

2.

本文中の知っておきたい単語は、オレンジの文字で記載しています。「Key Words」でその語句の解説も掲載しました。
また、知っておきたいイディオムや構文は、オレンジでマークしています。

3.

知っておきたいイディオムや構文の解説と、それを使った例文も掲載しています。

4.

本文で掲載しきれなかったものは「Other Expressions」で紹介しています。あなたを表現する英文をどんどん作りましょう。

本書の使い方

Contents

はじめに ———————————————— 2

第 1 章 家族

01 自己紹介 ———————————————— 12
02 ふるさと・出身地 ———————————— 16
03 住んでいる町 ————————————— 20
04 暮らしている家 ———————————— 24
05 両親 ————————————————— 30
06 兄弟・姉妹 ————————————— 34
07 子ども ———————————————— 38
08 学校 ————————————————— 44
09 学校の同窓会 ————————————— 50
10 恋人 ————————————————— 54
11 ペット ———————————————— 58

第 2 章 会社・仕事

12 採用面接 ——————————————— 64
13 会社で ———————————————— 68
14 人事部長との交渉(1) ————————— 74
15 人事部長との交渉(2) ————————— 78
16 通勤電車 ——————————————— 82
17 会社の飲み会にて ——————————— 88
18 転勤の辞令を拝受 ——————————— 92

第 3 章 日常生活

- 19 レストランで ……………… 98
- 20 カフェで ……………… 102
- 21 バーで ……………… 106
- 22 喫煙室で ……………… 112
- 23 ショッピングモールで ……………… 116
- 24 ショーウインドウの前で ……………… 120
- 25 ドライブにて ……………… 126
- 26 病院にて ……………… 130

第 4 章 趣味・価値観

- 27 機内で ……………… 136
- 28 映画館で ……………… 140
- 29 本屋で ……………… 144
- 30 英会話学校で ……………… 150
- 31 ジムで ……………… 154
- 32 習い事 ……………… 158
- 33 アウトドア ……………… 164
- 34 ビーチで ……………… 168
- 35 化粧 ……………… 172
- 36 ボランティア ……………… 178
- 37 女子会で ……………… 182
- 38 結婚観 ……………… 186

第1章 家族

Family

01 自己紹介

I've been a computer geek since I was a child.

子どもの頃からコンピューターオタクだったの。

Hi, my name's Yamada Eiko. I don't really like my name, since it's so plain. I'm 30 years old, and I work in IT as a website producer. Actually, I've been a computer geek since I was a child, so I think my job really suits me. I've always been devoted to my work, but I've managed to keep a balance between work and my personal life. Recently, though, the balance has definitely tipped towards work, and my family claims I've become a workaholic! What's worse, I noticed that I'm starting to develop a spare tire around my waist because of my bad eating habits. To get back in shape, I'm planning on getting up earlier and cycling to work. I've also started learning about organic foods and products so I can start eating healthier instead of stuffing my face with junk food. Some of my friends live abroad, so I keep in touch with them through Skype. Being a computer geek has its benefits!

Key Words

- geek：オタク、マニア
- be devoted to 〜：〜に専念する、没頭する
- manage to 〜：何とか〜する
- tip towards 〜：〜に傾く
- workaholic：仕事中毒(の人)※アルコール中毒からの造語
- a spare tire：(お腹の)贅肉
- because of 〜：〜が原因で、〜のために
- in shape：体調が良くて
- eat healthy：健康的な食事をする
- stuff one's face with 〜：〜を詰め込む
- keep in touch with 〜：〜と連絡を取る
- benefit：利点、特典

Translation

こんにちは、私の名前はヤマダエイコ。とても地味な名前だからあまり好きじゃないの。今、30歳でWEBプロデューサーとしてIT企業に勤務しているわ。実は、子どもの頃からコンピューターオタクだったから、この仕事は本当に私に合っていると思う。いつも仕事に没頭しているけど、何とか仕事と私生活のバランスをうまくとってきた。でも、最近、そのバランスが完全に仕事に傾いて、仕事中毒になっているよ、と家族から言われてしまう始末。もっと悪いことに、食習慣の乱れのせいか、腰の周りに贅肉がつき始めていることに気づいちゃった。元に戻すために、もっと早起きをして自転車通勤をしようかなと思っているの。あと、ジャンクフードを詰め込む代わりに、もっと健康的な食事が始められるよう、オーガニック食品とオーガニック製品の勉強をし始めたところ。海外で生活している友だちもいるから、スカイプで連絡を取っているの。コンピューターオタクにも特典ありっていうこと！

Point

☐ so I can start eating healthier.
　より健康的な食事が始められるように
　＊〜 so (that) S can… 〔Sが…するように、できるように〕

★ Jim studied hard so he could pass the exam.
　ジムは試験に合格するように一生懸命勉強した。

Other Expressions

❶ 私は1995年11月19日生まれ。
I was born on November 19, 1995.

❷ 私は13歳まで北海道育ちなの。
I was brought up in Hokkaido until I was 13 years old.

❸ 佐藤が名字でヒデキが名前。
Satoh is my family name and Hideki is my given name.

❹ この会社には勤続10年。
I've been working for this company for ten years.

❺ 営業部なんだ。
I work in the Sales Department.

❻ 明治大学の学生で、専攻は経済学。
I'm a student at Meiji University. I major in economics.

❼ 名前はケンジ。短くケンと呼んで。
My first name is Kenji. Please call me Ken for short.

❽ 父は私を美しい花に因んでユリと名付けた。
My father named me Yuri after a beautiful flower.

❾ 父親似とよく言われる。
I'm often told that I look like my father.

❿ 一青窈の大ファンで、彼女のことならほとんど何でも知ってるよ。
I'm a big fan of Hitoto Yo. I know almost everything about her.

02 ふるさと・出身地

It's quite a beautiful town.

とっても美しい町なんだ。

I was born in Mikawa in the Chichibu region of Saitama. You've probably never heard of it, because it's really small and in the middle of nowhere. There's only one post office, one supermarket, and one train station – it really is a one-horse town! It's such a rural place that the local high school is surrounded by rice fields. The town's population is barely a couple of thousand people, and most of them are retirees. But even though it's tiny and isolated, it's quite a beautiful town. It's close to nature, and the river is great for fishing. The town's most notable feature is an old shrine near the edge of town, which is reputed to be haunted! It's quite a gloomy place. My family has lived there for many generations, and my parents and grandparents are still there, so I visit Mikawa several times a year. But whenever I go there, I avoid the shrine, as I'm rather superstitious about ghosts…

Key Words

- region：地域
- in the middle of nowhere：何もない所に、人里離れた所に
- a one-horse town：過疎の寂れた町
- rural：田舎の
- barely：かろうじて、たったの〜
- retiree：定年退職者
- isolated：孤立した
- notable：注目すべき
- feature：特徴
- be reputed to 〜：〜だと言われている
- haunted：幽霊のよく出る
- gloomy：薄暗い
- avoid：避ける
- superstitious：迷信を信じる

Translation

僕は埼玉・秩父地方のミカワ生まれ。本当に小さくて、何もない所だから、たぶん一度も聞いたことがないんじゃないかな。郵便局とスーパーと鉄道の駅がそれぞれ1つずつあるだけで、本当に過疎の寂れた町。田舎町だから、地元の高校は田んぼに囲まれているんだ。町の人口は、たったの数千人で、大部分が定年退職者たち。でも、小さく孤立しても、とっても美しい町。町は自然に近く、川は釣りをするには最高だ。町の一番注目すべき特徴は町外れにある古い神社で、そこには幽霊がよく出るっていう話。とっても薄暗い所なんだ。僕の家族は何世代もその町に住んでいて、両親や祖父母はまだそこにいるから、年に数回ミカワを訪れている。でも、僕は幽霊の迷信をかなり信じているから、そこに行く時はいつも、その神社は避けて通っているんだ。

Point

☐ **Even though it's tiny and isolated, it's quite a beautiful town.**
小さく孤立しても、とっても美しい町。
＊ even though SV ～ ：{たとえでも}

★ **Even though he is the President, I won't change my mind.**
たとえ彼が大統領でも、私は考えを変えない。

Other Expressions

❶ 東京の浅草生まれだけど、13歳の時に埼玉へ転居。
I was born in Asakusa in Tokyo and my family moved to Saitama when I was 13 years old.

❷ 妻の故郷は岩手の海岸沿いにある小さな町。
My wife's hometown is a small town located on the coast of Iwate.

❸ 年に2回、故郷の両親を訪れる。
I visit my parents in my hometown twice a year.

❹ 月に1回は必ず墓参りに行く。
I make a point of visiting my ancestor's grave at least once a month.

❺ 私の故郷は山に囲まれた長野の小さな村。
My hometown is a small village in Nagano, surrounded by the mountains.

❻ 名古屋の生まれ故郷まで高速で5時間。
It takes five hours to get to my hometown in Nagoya on expressway.

❼ この曲を聴くと故郷を思い出すなぁ。
This music reminds me of my hometown.

❽ 今年の夏は、故郷に帰って1週間、両親と過ごす予定。
This summer I'm going back to my hometown to spend one week with my parents.

❾ 両親は私が行くのを楽しみにしているみたい。
It seems my parents are looking forward to my visit.

❿ 息子たちは祖父母に会うのを楽しみにしているわ。
My sons are looking forward to seeing their grand-parents.

03 住んでいる町

There are three subway lines that run through Sakura Station.

サクラ駅を通っている地下鉄の路線は3つあるわ。

I'm currently living in Sakura, near Tokyo. It's a lively city, with convenience stores and vending machines at every corner. There are three subway lines that run through Sakura Station, which makes travel very convenient. During the morning rush hour, the people in the subway cars are packed like sardines! My apartment is located near the National Sumo Wrestling Stadium, so I always see sumo wrestlers around town, loitering or cycling around. At first, it was a really odd sight, but I've become used to it by now. Strangely enough, I've never been to a sumo match in my life! Since the Sumo Wrestling Stadium is nearby, I often run into tourists who are lost. I don't know why, but they always ask me for directions! That's why I've had so many chances to brush up on my English. With so many sumo wrestlers and foreign people out and about, it's really an unusual place to live.

Key Words

- [ ] currently：今（のところ）
- [ ] lively：活気のある
- [ ] vending machine：自販機
- [ ] packed like sardines：すし詰め状態で
- [ ] loiter：ぶらぶらする
- [ ] odd：奇妙な
- [ ] become used to 〜：〜に慣れる
- [ ] strangely enough：不思議なことに
- [ ] run into 〜：〜に出くわす
- [ ] ask + 人 + for directions：人に道を尋ねる
- [ ] that's why SV 〜：そう言うわけで、だから
- [ ] brush up on 〜：〜に磨きをかける
- [ ] out and about：歩き回って

Translation

今は東京の近くのサクラに住んでいるわ。サクラは至る所にコンビニや自販機があって、活気ある都市。サクラ駅を通っている地下鉄の路線は3つあって、移動するのにとっても便利なのよ。朝のラッシュアワー時には、地下鉄の乗客たちはすし詰め状態。私のアパートは国技館の近くにあるから、相撲取りたちが町をブラブラしたり、自転車に乗ったりしているのをいつも目にするの。最初は実に奇妙な光景だったけど、もう慣れちゃった。不思議なことに、今まで一回も相撲の試合に行ったことがないの。国技館が近いから、道に迷った観光客によく会うのよね。なぜだかわからないけれど、いつも道を聞かれるの。だから英語に磨きをかける機会がたくさんあるわ。相撲取りや外国人たちがたくさん歩き回っているから、住むには本当に変わったところなのよ。

Point

- **I always see sumo wrestlers around town, loitering or cycling around.**
  町中で相撲取りたちがブラブラしたり、自転車に乗っているのをいつも目にします。
  * see + O + ~ing {Oが〜しているのを見る、目にする}

★ **I saw them playing tennis.**
彼らがテニスをしているのを見た。

Other Expressions

❶ 閑静な住宅街に住みたい。
I want to live in a quiet residential area.

❷ この都市の人口は約20万人。
The population of this city is about 200,000.

❸ 私たちの町はせんべいで有名。
Our town is famous for its rice crackers.

❹ 私のアパートから会社まで電車で約1時間。
It's about one- hour train ride from my apartment to the office.

❺ この都市には3つの地下鉄と2つの鉄道の駅がある。
There are three subway lines and two train stations in this city.

❻ 最寄り駅周辺にはたくさんの飲み屋があるなぁ。
There are many bars around the nearest station.

❼ 市の中心に大きな川が流れている。
There's a big river running through the middle of the city.

❽ 駅の周辺にはたくさんの高層マンションが建設中。
Many high-rise condominiums are being constructed around the station.

❾ この都市の人口はここ数年、増え続けているわ。
The population of this city has been increasing for the past few years.

❿ 町外れに大きなショッピングモールが建設中。
A big shopping mall is under construction on the outskirts of town.

04 暮らしている家

I have mixed feelings about my apartment.

アパートの善し悪しについては複雑な気持ちだわ。

I have mixed feelings about my apartment. On one hand, it's very close to my workplace, it is right next to the subway station, and the rent is reasonable. On the other hand, the building is so run-down that it's falling apart, my neighbors are very noisy, and the apartment is only six tatami mats large! Yesterday, I came home and my apartment's front door knob broke when I tried to open it. I had to call the superintendent and wait outside for two hours until he fixed it. And last week, the kitchen sink's faucet broke and flooded half of my apartment. I had to throw away dozens of books and magazines that were ruined because of the water damage. The straw that broke the camel's back is the fact that the landlord wants to raise the rent! The landlord claims the higher rent will be used to pay for repairs in the building, but I don't believe it. I've started hunting for a new apartment, but I still haven't found one with affordable rent and a convenient location.

Key Words

- run-down：荒廃した
- fall apart：崩壊する
- superintendent：管理人
- faucet：蛇口
- flood：水浸しにする
- dozens of ～：数十の～
- ruin：ダメにする
- the straw that breaks the camel's back
  ：我慢の限度を超えさせるもの
- landlord：大家
- repairs：修理
- affordable：手ごろな

Translation

アパートの善し悪しについては複雑な気持ちだわ。一方で、職場にとても近くて、地下鉄の駅のすぐ隣だし、家賃も手ごろ。他方、建物は荒廃し崩れ落ちそうで、隣人たちもうるさくて、アパートの部屋もたったの6畳ほどの大きさしかないの。昨日、帰宅してドアを開けようとしたら、玄関のドアノブが壊れちゃったの。管理人を呼んで直してもらうまで2時間も外で待たなければならなかったわ。そして先週、キッチンの流しの蛇口が壊れて、部屋の半分が水浸しに。水害でダメになった数十冊の本と雑誌を捨てなければならなくなったの。どうしても我慢できないのは、大家さんが家賃を上げたがっていること。家賃を上げて、建物の修理代に使うと大家さんは言っているけれど、そんなことは信じないわ。新しいアパートを探し始めているけれど、手ごろな家賃と便利な立地条件の物件は未だに見つかっていないの。

Point

☐ **I still haven't found one with affordable rent and a convenient location.**

手ごろな家賃と便利な立地条件の物件は未だに見つかってない。

* still not 〜「まだ〜していない」not 〜 yet も「まだ〜していない」の意味であるが、後者が単なる事実を伝えているだけなのに対して、前者は「苛立ちの気持ち」が含まれる。

↓

★ **He still hasn't turned up.**

彼はまだ来てないの。

Other Expressions

❶ 職場に近い別のアパートに引っ越ししようかな。

I'm thinking of moving to another apartment near my workplace.

❷ あんな大きなマンションに住めたらなあ。

I wish I could live in such a big condominium.

❸ 彼のアパートの間取りは、寝室が1部屋とリビングと浴室とキッチン。

His apartment is made up of one bedroom, one living room, one bathroom, and one kitchen.

❹ アパート暮らしを一度もしたことがないの。一人暮らししてみたい。

I've never lived in an apartment. I want to live by myself.

❺ うちの家族は来月、東京の郊外のベッドタウンに引っ越す予定。

My family is moving to a commuter town in the suburbs of Tokyo next month.

❻ 駅から5分以内で、日当たりのいい部屋がいいなあ。

I want a room with a lot of sun and within 5 minutes' walk of the station.

❼ あのアパートはエアコン付かなあ？

Is that apartment equipped with an air conditioner?

❽ そろそろ壁紙を張り替えないと。

It's about time I repapered the walls.

❾ 引っ越しの準備は大変。

It's hard preparing for this move.

❿ この箱重い。何が入っているのかな？

This box is too heavy. What's inside?

What can you do to promote world peace?
Go home and love your family.
– Mother Teresa

世界平和のために、あなたにできることですか？
家に帰って、家族を愛してあげることです。
マザー・テレサ

05 両親

It wasn't love at first sight.

一目惚れじゃなかった。

My parents are an unusual couple. My father is a grocer and my mother is a housewife, but that's not what makes them so strange! My father is 20 years older than my mother. My father met my mother when she graduated from college and started working at my father's supermarket. My father says she was so beautiful, he fell head over heels in love with her! My mother, however, says it wasn't love at first sight. She says my father was a very strict boss so she was very frightened of him. He might have been strict when he was younger, but he has mellowed with age. My mother is quite small and wears eyeglasses. Everyone says she would be very pretty if she didn't have to wear such thick lenses. She always has her nose in a book, and she especially loves to read mystery novels. When she is reading an interesting story, she neglects the housework, but my father never complains. He just makes me do it instead!

Key Words

- □ unusual：変わった、まれな
- □ grocer：食品雑貨商
- □ graduate from 〜：〜を卒業する
- □ fall head over heels in love with 〜：〜にぞっこんである
- □ love at first sight：一目ぼれ
- □ be frightened of 〜：〜を怖がる
- □ mellow：丸くなる
- □ have one's nose in a book：本に熱中する、本の虫である
- □ mystery novel：推理小説
- □ neglect：怠る

Translation

両親は変わった夫婦なんだ。父は食品雑貨商で母は主婦だけど、彼らを変わった夫婦にしているのはそんなことじゃない。父は母より20歳年上なんだ。父が母に出会ったのは、母が大学を卒業して父のスーパーマーケットで働き始めた時。母はとても美人だからぞっこんだったと父は言っている。でも、母の方は一目ぼれではなかったと言っているんだ。母が言うには、父はとても厳しい上司だったから母はとても怖がっていたみたい。父は若いころは厳しかったみたいだけど、年齢と共に丸くなった。母はかなり小柄で眼鏡をかけている。そんなに分厚いレンズをつけなくてもいいなら、とっても可愛いのに、とみんなは言っている。彼女はいつも本の虫で、特に推理小説を読むのが大好き。面白いものを読んでいる時は家事を怠けるけど、父は決して文句は言わない。その代わり、僕が家事をさせられるんだ。

Point

☐ **She would be very pretty if she didn't have to wear such thick lenses.**
そんな分厚いレンズをつけなくていいならとっても可愛いのに。
＊過去形を使って現在の事実を仮定・願望する表現

★ **Life would be easier if we didn't have to pay the debt.**
借金を払わなくてもよければ生活はもっと楽なのに。

Other Expressions

❶ まだ両親のすねをかじってるの。
   I'm still dependent on my parents.

❷ 彼は両親からはすでに独立しているわ。
   He's already independent of his parents.

❸ 両親はまだ元気でぴんぴんしてるの。
   My parents are still alive and kicking.

❹ 父は55歳の時に癌で他界。
   My father died of cancer at the age of 55.

❺ 母は99歳まで生きたわ。
   My mother lived to be 99 years old.

❻ 父が亡くなったら私が財産を相続することになっているの。
   I'm supposed to inherit my father's property after his death.

❼ 両親は年金だけで生活しているわ。
   My parents live on their pension alone.

❽ 母は5年前に肺がんになったけど今は元気。
   My mother came down with lung cancer but now she is fine.

❾ 両親が一緒に住めるように改築をするつもり。
   I'm going to remodel our house so that my parents can live with us.

❿ 父はかつて、JALのパイロットだった。
   My father used to be a pilot for JAL.

06 兄弟・姉妹

She is usually very mild-mannered, but…

普段、彼女はとても温和だけど…

I have two siblings, a younger sister and an older brother. My younger sister Mio is in her junior year of high school. She's a member of the brass band, and plays the sax. Her club practices six days a week, so she's always complaining that she is too busy. Since she is the youngest member of the family, she is a bit spoiled. She is usually very mild-mannered, but she becomes angry if she cannot get what she wants. When my father refused to buy her a smart phone, she threw a real hissy fit! She wouldn't calm down until my father said he would reconsider. My brother Kotaro is very different from my sister. He works at a trading company, and was recently promoted due to his hard work. My brother loves to go to karaoke to sing old rock songs. Unfortunately, he's completely tone-deaf and his singing voice is absolutely awful! Once, I teased my sister and told her she and my brother should form a musical duo, and she got really upset with me.

Key Words

- sibling：(男女の区別のない)きょうだい
- junior year：高校1年生
- complain：不平を言う
- spoiled：甘やかされた
- mild-mannered：温和な
- throw a real hissy fit：本気になって怒る
- calm down：落ち着く
- reconsider：考え直す
- unfortunately：残念ながら、不運にも
- tone-deaf：音痴の
- tease：からかう
- get upset with 〜：〜に腹を立てる

Translation

私には2人のきょうだい、妹と兄がいるの。妹のミオは高校1年生。彼女は吹奏楽部のメンバーで、サックスを吹いているの。部活動は週に6日なので、いつも忙しいと不平を言っているわ。末っ子だから、ちょっと甘やかされているのよ。普段はとても温和だけど、欲しいものが手に入らないと短気になるの。父がスマートフォンを買うのを拒んだら、本気でかんしゃくを起こしていたもの。父が考え直すと言うまでは冷静になろうとはしなかったのよ。兄のコウタロウは妹とは大違い。彼は商社に勤めていて、勤勉さゆえに最近、昇進したの。兄はカラオケに行って昔のロックの歌を歌うのが大好き。残念ながら、彼は完ぺきな音痴で、歌声は全くひどいもの。昔、妹をからかって、兄とデュオを組めば、と言ったら、妹は本気になって私に腹を立てていたわ。

Point

☐ **He was recently promoted due to his hard work.**
彼は最近、勤勉さゆえに昇進した。
 ＊due to ～「～が原因で、～のために」同じ意味の慣用句に、because of ～、on account of ～、owing to ～などがある。

★ **The train was delayed due to the heavy snow.**
大雪のために列車が遅れた。

Other Expressions

❶ 私は一人っ子だから、きょうだいがいたらなあ。
Since I'm an only child, I wish I had siblings.

❷ 私には2人兄弟がいるけど、2人とも結婚してる。
I have two brothers, both of whom are married.

❸ 妹は美しい花に因んでユリと名付けられたの。
My younger sister was named Yuri after a beautiful flower.

❹ 私には3歳年上の兄がいるわ。
I have a brother, who is older than me by three years.

❺ 彼女は父親似かな、それとも母親似かな？
Does she take after her father, or her mother?

❻ 彼らは双子だけど、あまり似ていないなあ。
They don't look very much alike, though they are twins.

❼ 彼女は何人きょうだいなのかな？
How many siblings does she have?

❽ 弟は野球チームに入っていて、3塁を守っているの。
My younger brother is on a baseball team and is at third base.

❾ 両親はいつも私とお姉ちゃんを比較ばかりしている。
My parents are always comparing me with my older sister.

❿ 2歳年下の弟とよく口げんかをするなあ。
Once in a while, I have a quarrel with my brother, who is two years younger than me.

07 子ども

Mrs. Kawamura has watched out for me like a mother.

川村さんは母親のように僕を見守ってくれているんだ。

Ever since I was hired at my company, Mrs. Kawamura has watched out for me like a mother hen taking care of a chick. She was telling me about her two kids. She has a 5-year-old boy named Kanji, and a 10-year-old named Daisuke. Kanji is very sweet, but a bit rowdy. She says he recently decided to make a painting in his bedroom, so he drew cartoon characters all over his bedroom walls using color markers. When Mrs. Kawamura got home, she really blew her top! She made him scrub all the drawings off the walls and took away all his markers. Then, she told him he wasn't allowed to watch TV for a week as punishment. She told me we sometimes have to be very strict with kids, or they will never learn discipline. Her oldest son, Daisuke, sounds like he's very good at foreign languages. He's a studious and gentle boy, and his fondest wish is to have a pet dog. Mrs. Kawamura doesn't want to get him a dog, because she thinks it would take time away from his studies! I wonder if that's a little too strict…

Key Words

- watch out for 〜：見守る、世話をする
- hen：雌鳥(めんどり)
- chick：ヒヨコ
- rowdy：乱暴な、騒々しい
- cartoon character：漫画の登場人物
- blow one's top：激怒する
- scrub：ごしごし洗う
- take away 〜：〜を奪う、持ち去る
- be allowed to 〜：〜するのを許される
- punishment：罰
- discipline：しつけ、規律
- studious：勉強好きな
- fondest：fond(優しい、楽しい)の最上級

Translation

会社に就職してからずっと、川村さんはヒヨコの面倒を見る雌鶏(めんどり)の母のように僕の世話をしてくれている。彼女は僕に2人の子供のことを話してくれた。彼女には5歳のカンジという男の子と10歳のダイスケという男の子がいる。カンジはとてもかわいいけれど、ちょっと利かん坊。彼は最近、寝室に絵を描こうと、カラーマーカーを使って寝室の壁中に漫画のキャラクターを描いた、と彼女は言う。帰宅すると、川村さんは激怒した。彼女は壁の絵を全部消させて、マーカーを全部取り上げた。それから、罰として1週間テレビを観てはいけないと彼に言ったんだ。時に子供には厳しくしないと決して規律を学ぶことがない、と彼女は僕に言った。長男のダイスケは外国語がとても得意という話。彼は勉強好きな優しい子で、今一番の希望は犬を買う(飼う)こと。川村さんが彼に犬を買ってあげたくないと思っているのは、勉強時間が取られてしまうと考えているから。ちょっと厳しすぎるんじゃないかな？

Point

☐ She made him scrub all the drawings off the walls.

彼女は彼に壁の絵を全部消させた。
* make + O + ～動詞の原形 {Oに～させる} Oに強制的にさせる場合に使う表現。
 let + O + ～動詞の原形 {Oに～させてやる}
 have + O + ～動詞の原形 {Oに～してもらう}

↓

★ The teacher made his student stand up.

先生は生徒を立たせた。

Other Expressions

❶ 娘の外見は私似。
My daughter takes after me in appearance.

❷ 息子の性格は私似。
My son takes after me in character.

❸ 息子はいっつもテレビゲームばかりしている。
My son is always playing video games.

❹ 娘は目の中に入れても痛くないわ。
My daughter is the apple of my eye.

❺ 娘は一人で生活したがっているが私は反対よ。
My daughter wants to find her own place, but I disagree.

❼ 長男は今、小学校3年生。
My oldest son is in the third grade.

❽ 一番下の娘は東京の私立高校に通っているの。
My youngest daughter goes to a private high school in Tokyo.

❾ 息子の将来の夢は外国で就職すること。
My son's dream for the future is to work abroad.

❿ 娘には国立大学に行ってもらいたいなあ。
I'd like my daughter to go on to a national university.

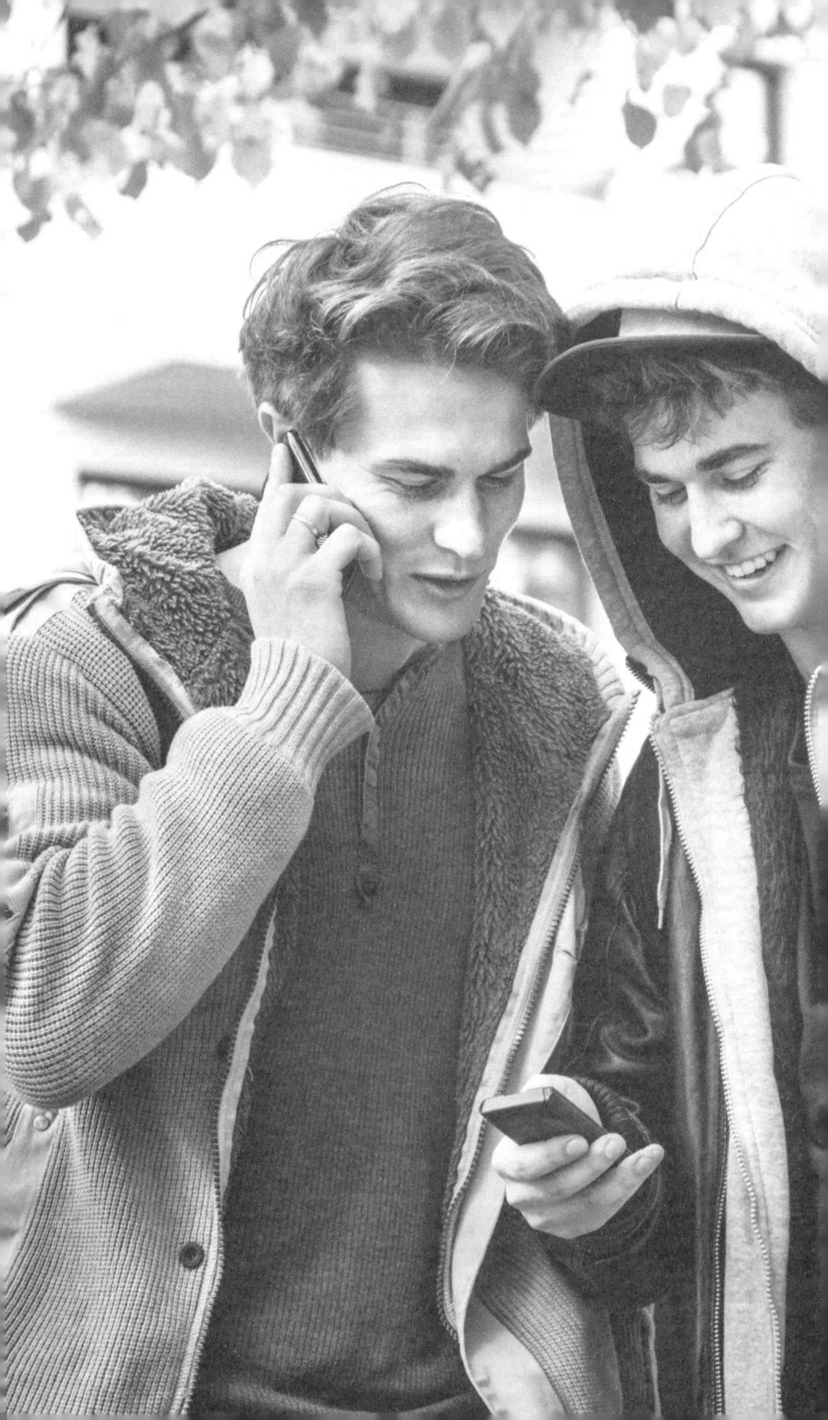

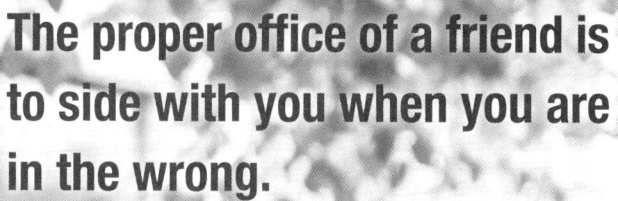

The proper office of a friend is to side with you when you are in the wrong.

- Mark Twain

あなたが間違っていても
味方してくれるのが
友だちっていうもの。
　　　　マーク・トウェイン

08 学校

My head was filled with memories of all my old classmates.

頭の中は昔の級友たちとの想い出で一杯だった。

Tonight, I'm going to my old high school's reunion. I was happily surprised when I received the invitation! I suddenly felt very nostalgic. My head was filled with memories of all my old classmates. I wonder what Ayaka is up to these days? I remember she was the most beautiful girl in our class. We all thought she would move to Paris and become a model after graduation. And what about Seiya? He was always cracking jokes and annoying the teachers. I remember that Ayaka couldn't stand him because he always disrupted our lessons. They were always arguing with each other. I also remember Takeru. He was our class president, and he came from a wealthy family. He always said that his ideas would make him rich before he was thirty years old. I wonder if he really became wealthy. Maybe Takeru could give me some good tips on investing in the stock market. I hope he comes to the reunion. I guess I will find out tonight! I'm really looking forward to it.

Key Words

- reunion：同窓会
- nostalgic：郷愁的な、懐かしい
- graduation：卒業
- crack jokes：冗談を飛ばす
- annoy：怒らせる
- stand：(否定文で)我慢できない
- disrupt：かき乱す
- argue：言い争う
- class president：学級委員長
- wealthy：裕福な
- tips：ヒント、アドバイス
- invest in 〜：〜に投資する
- stock market：株式市場
- find out：わかる

Translation

今夜は高校時代の同窓会に行く予定なんだ。招待状をもらった時は嬉しい驚きだったな！　急に懐かしくなっちゃった。頭の中は昔の級友たちとの想い出で一杯だった。今、アヤカはどうしているかなあ。覚えているのは、彼女はクラスで一番の美人だったこと。卒業後はパリへ行ってモデルになるとみんな思っていたなあ。それに、セイヤはどうしてるかな。彼はいつも冗談を飛ばして先生たちを怒らせていたっけ。いつも授業をかき乱していたから、アヤカはセイヤには我慢がならないっていうのを覚えてる。二人はいつも言い争っていたなあ。タケルのことも覚えてる。彼は学級委員長で、裕福な家の出だった。30歳までにはアイデアを駆使して金持ちになるといつも言っていた。本当に金持ちになったのかなあ。たぶん、タケルは株式の投資に関する良いアドバイスをしてくれるんじゃないかなあ。彼が来てくれるといいんだけど。今夜わかると思う。本当に楽しみだなあ。

Point

☐ **I'm really looking forward to it.**
本当に楽しみだな。
  * looking forward to 〜 {〜を楽しみにする}
    to は前置詞なので「〜」には名詞もしくは動名詞が続く。

↓

★ **I'm looking forward to seeing you again.**
また会えるのを楽しみにしている。

Other Expressions

❶ 大学時代の専攻は法学。
I majored in law in college.

❷ 出身大学は北海道大学。
I graduated from Hokkaido University.

❸ 彼はどこの学校に行っているのかな？
Where does he go to school?

❹ 放課後は近所のガソリンスタンドでアルバイトしたなあ。
I used to work part-time at a gas station nearby.

❺ 週に3回、ピアノのレッスンを受けていたわ。
I took piano lessons three times a week.

❻ 高校3年生のころは毎日塾通い。
I went to cram school every day when I was in my senior year of high school.

❼ 担任の先生は剣道部の顧問だったの。
My homeroom teacher was in charge of the Kendo club.

❽ 僕が通っていた高校は田んぼに囲まれていたんだ。
My high school was surrounded by rice fields.

❾ あの歌手は私と同じ中学の出身。
That singer is from the same junior high school as me.

❿ 学校には数人の交換留学生がいたわ。
We had some foreign exchange students in our school.

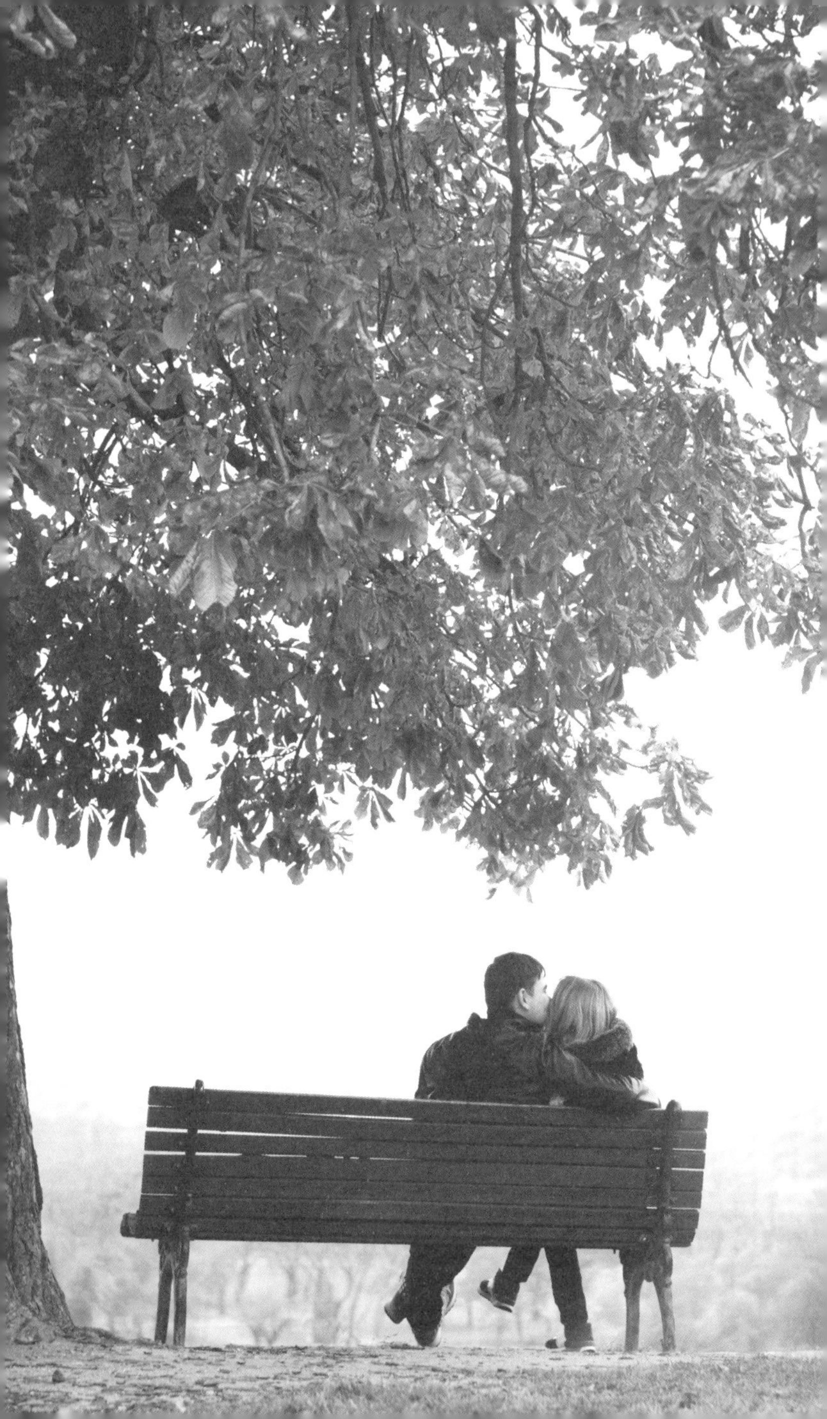

Life is an exciting business and most exciting when it is lived for others.

- Helen Keller

人生は胸おどるもの。
そして一番ワクワクするのは人のために生きたとき。
ヘレンケラー

09 学校の同窓会

I went to my high school's reunion tonight.

今夜、高校時代の同窓会に行ってきたんだ。

I went to my high school's reunion tonight. It was great to catch up with friends and classmates I hadn't seen in a long time. Ayaka, who used to be so popular, is now married with five kids! I think having so many children has been difficult for her. She has a few gray hairs and looks tired. Still, she's very proud of her kids – she boasted about them to everyone! Her husband is Seiya, who was the class clown. These days he's a serious-looking salaryman. Takeru, our former class president, is now trying to find investors for a start-up company. He was asking everyone if they wanted to invest money in his company…he even begged me for some cash! He must be desperate.

Key Words

- catch up with 〜：〜と久しぶりに会って話をする
- be married with 〜：結婚して〜がいる
- boast about 〜：〜を自慢する
- salaryman：サラリーマン※この単語は元々は和製英語であったが、現在では、特に長時間働く日本の会社員のことを言う
- former：前の、元の
- investor：投資家
- start-up：始めたばかりの
- beg：乞う
- desperate：必死の

Translation

今夜、高校時代の同窓会に行ってきた。長い間会っていなかった友だちや級友たちと、久しぶりに会って話すのは最高だった。昔とても人気があったアヤカは、今は結婚して子供が5人。そんなに子供がいたら大変だろうなあ。白髪が少しあって疲れているように見えた。でも、子供たちを誇りに思っていて、みんなに自慢していたなぁ。彼女の夫は、クラスのお調子者だったセイヤ。今では真面目そうなサラリーマンになっていた。元学級委員のタケルは目下、始めたばかりの会社に投資してくれる人を探しているところだった。会社に投資してくれないかとみんなに頼んでいたな。彼は、僕に金の無心すらしてきたんだ。彼は必死に違いない。

Point

☐ Ayaka, who used to be so popular, is now married with five kids!

昔とても人気があったアヤカは今は結婚して子供が5人！

* used to ～〔昔～だった〕過去の習慣や状態を表し、現在ではそうでないことを暗示している。たとえば、I used to smoke.〔昔は煙草を吸っていた〕は、今は煙草をやめていることを示している。

↓

★ There used to be a bank in front of the station.

昔は駅前に銀行があった。

Other Expressions

❶ 来週の同窓会が待ち遠しいなあ。
I can hardly wait for the school reunion next week.

❷ 高校を卒業してから、もう30年。
It's already been 30 years since I graduated from high school.

❸ 高校時代はサッカーチームに入っていたよ。
I was on the soccer team when I was in high school.

❹ 頭が禿げたあの男性は一体、誰？
Who on earth is that man with bald head?

❺ あの太った女性はもしかしたら昔付き合ってたジュンコかなあ？
Is that fat woman Junko by any chance, whom I used to go out with?

❻ 見覚えのない人たちが多いなあ。
There are so many people I can't recognize.

❼ 担任の坂田先生は全然変わってないな。
Our homeroom teacher, Mr. Sakata, hasn't changed at all.

❽ クラス会は東京の一流ホテルで行われたんだ。
The class reunion was held in a first-rate hotel in Tokyo.

❾ 会の最後に校歌を歌って終えたよ。
We ended up singing our school song.

❿ 5年後に再会することを約束したの。
We promised to meet again in five years.

10 恋人

I love her, but she's a bit childish sometimes.

彼女を愛してるけど、ちょっと子供すぎる時がある。

Oh, no, another missed call from my girlfriend, Karen! This is the fifth one today. Unfortunately, she never leaves a message on my cell phone, so I never know if her calls are urgent or not. I can't call her until I finish working. Whenever she's on the phone with me, she talks my ear off. If I tell her I'm busy, she gets upset and accuses me of wanting to hang up on her! I love her, but she's a bit childish sometimes. She always wants me to pay attention to her, even when I don't have the time. Please don't think she's a bad person. When I'm sick, she takes time off work and comes to visit me, cooks for me, and makes sure I take my medicine. When I broke my toe, she even drove me to the doctor's office, even though I knew she had tickets for a K-Pop concert! My mother tells me that Karen is quite a catch. She says I should propose to her soon. When I told Karen what my mother had said, can you guess what her reaction was? She said, "Your mother is a very wise woman!"

Key Words

- [ ] missed call：電話に出そこなうこと
- [ ] cell phone：携帯電話
- [ ] urgent：緊急な
- [ ] talk one's ear off：何度も同じことを聞いて耳にタコができる
- [ ] accuse + O + of ～：～のことでOを責める、非難する
- [ ] hang up on ～：話し終わらないうちに～からの電話を切る
- [ ] pay attention to ～：～に注意を向ける
- [ ] take time off work：仕事を休む
- [ ] catch：めっけもの

Translation

ああダメだ、またガールフレンドのカレンからの電話に出られなかった。今日はこれで5回目。あいにく、彼女は絶対に僕のケータイにメッセージを残さないから、緊急な電話かどうかわからないよ。仕事が終わるまでは、僕から彼女に電話ができないし。彼女と電話で話をする時は、いつも同じことばかり言うから、もう耳にタコができそうだよ。忙しいと言うと腹を立てて、僕が電話を切りたがっているととがめるし。彼女を愛しているけど、ちょっと子供すぎる時があるんだよなあ。僕に時間がない時でも、常に自分の方を向いてほしいと思っているんだ。でも、彼女を悪い人だとは思わないでほしい。僕が病気の時は、仕事を休んで見舞いに来て料理を作り、薬を飲み忘れないようにしてくれるんだ。足の指を骨折した時も、病院まで車で連れて行ってくれたし。彼女がKポップのコンサートチケットを持っていることを知っていたんだけどね（チケットを持っていたのに、助けてくれた）。カレンは中々のめっけものと母は僕に言う。すぐにプロポーズしろとも言う。母が言ったことを彼女に話したら、彼女の反応はどうだったと思う？「あなたのお母さんは賢い女性ね」これが彼女の答えだった。

Point

☐ **She makes sure I take my medicine.**
彼女は僕が薬を飲むのを忘れないようにしてくれる。
＊ make sure SV～ {Sが～するように（注意）する、Sが～することを確認する}

⬇

★ **Make sure you call me at noon.**
忘れずに正午に電話してください。

Other Expressions

❶ 彼に一目惚れしちゃったの。
I fell in love with him at first sight.

❷ こんな気持ち初めて。
I've never felt this way before.

❸ 彼に初めて会った時のこと忘れないわ。
I'll never forget the first time I met him.

❹ また彼女に会えるなんて夢みたい。
It's like a dream come true to be able to see her again.

❺ 彼女はまさに僕のタイプ。
She's just my type.

❻ 初めて彼に会った時、ドキドキしちゃった。
My heart was pounding when I saw him for the first time.

❼ 夕べ、彼から告白されたの。
Last night he told me he loves me.

❽ 初恋なの。
This is the first time I've been in love.

❾ 近頃、彼女のことばかり考えてる。
I've been thinking about her lately.

❿ 彼はきっと運命の人だわ。
I'm sure he's my destiny.

11 ペット

I've been thinking about getting a pet.

ペットを買おう（飼おう）か考えているの。

These days, when I walk home from work, I always stop in front of the pet store. Looking at the puppies and kittens in the display window always warms my heart. I've been thinking about getting a pet for a while now, but I'm worried I wouldn't have time to take care of it properly. I've been too busy at the office lately. It seems there's always a new crisis or emergency just when I'm about to leave, and I always end up staying late. Still, now that I'm living by myself, a dog or a cat would make good company. Which would be better? A dog would give me an excuse to get up earlier, take it for a walk, and get good exercise. And dogs can be trained very easily, too. But a dog is a very social animal, and it would be very lonely cooped up alone in the house all day. Perhaps a cat would be better. Cats are very independent creatures and they can live quite happily on their own for most of the day. But, to be honest, I like dogs more than cats! Dogs are so much friendlier, and cuter! Oh, what should I do? I can't decide! Maybe I should just buy a fish…

Key Words

- puppy：子犬
- kitten：子猫
- display window：ショーウインドウ
- for a while：しばらく
- take care of 〜：〜の世話をする
- properly：きちんと
- crisis：危機
- emergency：緊急
- end up 〜 ing：結局〜に終わる
- make good company：仲良くなる
- excuse：口実、言い訳
- train：訓練する
- coop up：とじこめる
- independent：独立した
- creature：生きもの
- on one's own：自分で、一人で
- to be honest：正直に言うと

Translation

最近、仕事から歩いて帰る途中に、ペットショップの前で必ず足を止めてしまうの。ショーウインドウの子犬や子猫を見るといつも心が温まるの。しばらくペットを買おうか（飼おうか）思案しているのだけれど、ちゃんと世話をする時間が取れるのかが心配だわ。最近、仕事が忙しすぎるの。ちょうど会社を出ようとする時に、新たな一大事や緊急事態があって、結局いつも遅くまでいることになってしまうの。でも、一人暮らしだから犬や猫は良い友だちになるかもしれない。どっちがいいかしら。犬ならもっと早く起きて散歩に連れて行って十分な運動をする口実になるかもしれない。それに、犬はしつけをするのも簡単だわ。でも、犬は社会的な生き物だから、一日中家に閉じ込められたらとても寂しいかもしれないわね。たぶん、猫の方が良いかな。猫はとっても独立心の強い動物だし、一日の大部分を一人で過ごしても、まあまあ楽しく過ごせるしね。でも、正直に言うと猫より犬の方が好きなんだ。犬の方がずっと人懐こいし、かわいい。ああ、どうすればいいの？　決められないわ。もしかしたら、魚の方がいいかしら。

Point

☐ Now that I'm living by myself, a dog or a cat would make good company.
一人暮らしだから犬や猫は良い友だちになるかも。
* Now that SV 〜,｛(今は) 〜だから、〜なので｝

↓

★ Now that she has gone, I can't see her any longer.
彼女は行ってしまったから、もう彼女には会えない。

Other Expressions

❶ アパート暮らしだから、ペットは飼えないの。
Since I live in an apartment, I can't have a pet.

❷ ペットが飼えたらなあ。
I wish I could have a pet.

❸ なんて可愛いネコ。
What a cute cat it is!

❹ この犬、ペットショップで衝動買いしちゃった。
I bought this dog on impulse at a pet shop.

❺ この子犬はどれくらい大きくなるのかな？
How big does this puppy grow?

❻ 熱帯魚にエサをあげるの忘れちゃった。
I forgot to feed the tropical fish.

❼ こんな可愛い子猫を見たのは初めて。
This is the first time I've seen this pretty cat.

❽ この犬は何歳くらいかな。
I wonder how old this dog is.

❾ 子犬たちと遊んでいる時が一番幸せ。
I feel happiest when I'm playing with the puppies.

❿ うちの犬はお客さんが来ると嬉しくて興奮するの。
My dog goes wild with excitement when someone visits me.

第2章 会社・仕事

Business

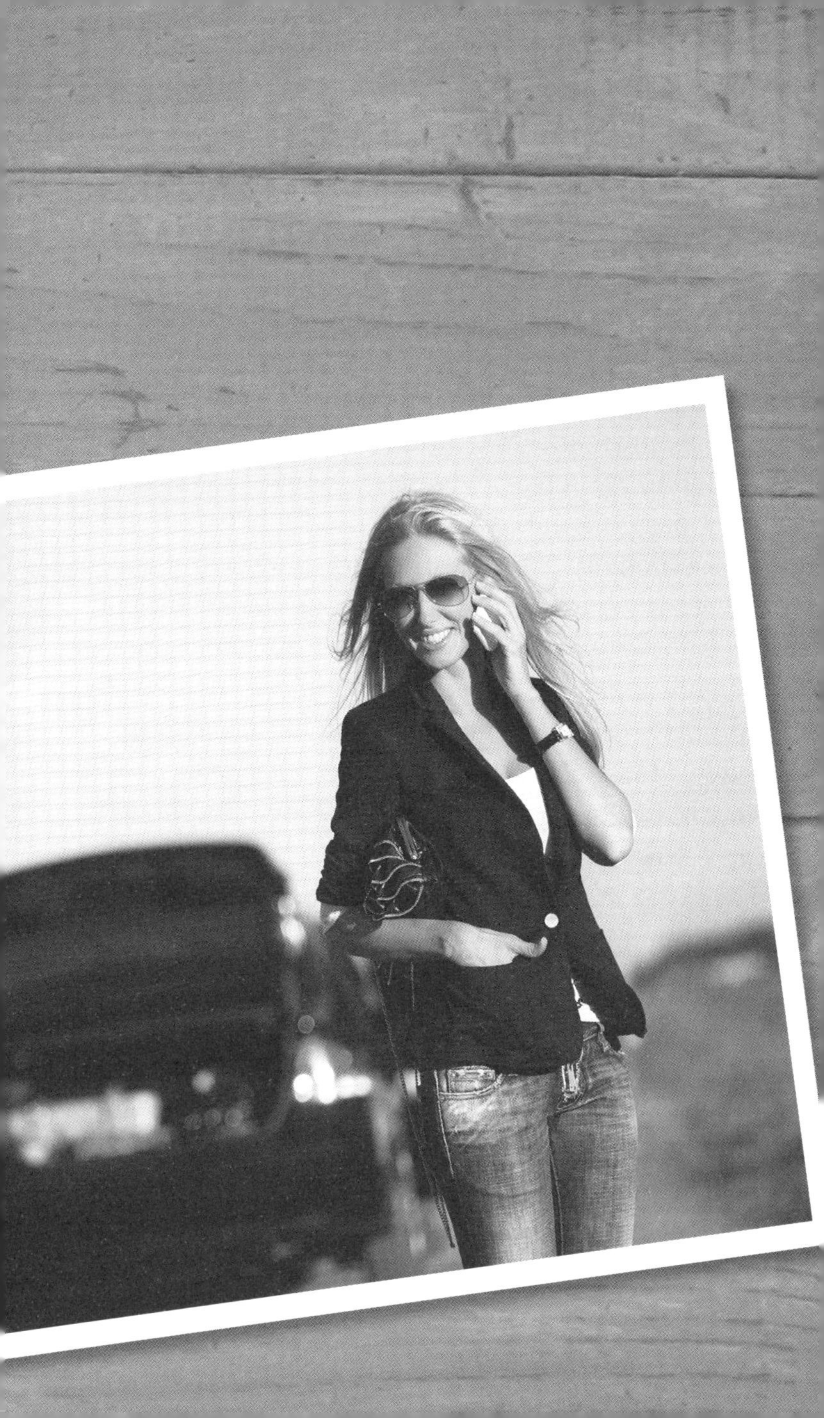

12 採用面接

My big job interview is today.

大事な面接の試験が今日あるんだ。

Oh, boy, my big job interview is today. Mrs. Kawamura and Mr. Satoh are going to be interviewing me today. My hands won't stop shaking! If I pass this interview, I'll be officially hired by the company. It's been a very long and arduous process to get to this point. I sent out so many job applications and took so many tests, and now I'm finally reaching my goal. I should remember the points that I want to stress during today's interview! First, I want them to see what assets I will bring to the company: my skills with computers, my English ability, and my prior experience working in an IT company. Of course, it's not my fault that my last company went bankrupt. It was really unlucky for me, but I was just an intern back then. I shouldn't think about that! Those are negative thoughts! Let's see, I should also tell them that I'm a hard worker, that I learn new things quickly, and that I don't mind working late. Oh, but not too late! I don't want to miss the last train…maybe I shouldn't mention that last part. Okay, I think I'm just about ready for my interview. Wish me luck!

Key Words

- hire：雇う
- arduous：困難な
- job application：エントリーシート
- stress：強調する
- asset：強み
- prior：前の
- go bankrupt：破産する
- intern：見習い、研修生
- mention：示唆する
- Wish me luck：うまく行くように祈っておいてね

Translation

ああ！ 今日は大事な面接の試験があるんだ。川村さんと佐藤さんが今日の僕の面接官の予定。両手の震えが止まらないよ！ この面接に合格したら、会社から正式に採用されることになる。ここまでは、とても長く困難な道のりだった。エントリーシートを本当にたくさん送ったし、試験もたくさん受けた。そして今、やっとゴールにたどり着こうとしている。今日の面接で強調したい点をいくつか思い出しておこう。まずは、僕が会社にもたらす強みが何であるかを見てもらいたい。コンピューターの技術なり、英語の能力なり、以前ＩＴ企業で働いていた実績なりをね。もちろん、前の会社が倒産したのは僕のせいじゃない。僕にとっては本当にアンラッキーだったけど、あの頃は見習いだったしね。そんなことは考えない方がいいか。マイナス思考だな！ ええっと、僕が働き者だってこと、物覚えが早いこと、そして、遅くまで働くことをいとわないことなどを伝えた方がいいかな。ああ、でも遅すぎるのはダメだ。終電に乗り遅れたくないから、最後の部分を言うのはやめておこう。ＯＫ、面接試験の準備はできた。うまく行くように祈っておいてね。

Point

☐ **It's not my fault that my last company went bankrupt.**
前の会社が倒産したのは私のせいじゃない。
  * It is not…that～ 〔～なのは…じゃない〕強調したい語（句）
    …の中に入れる構文

↓

★ **It's not you that are to blame.**
悪いのは君じゃない。

Other Expressions

❶ 今から会社訪問だよ。
I'm going on a company visit.

❷ 先月から就活中なんだ。
I've been looking for a job since last month.

❸ 何社回ったか覚えていないよ。
I don't remember how many companies I visited.

❹ エントリーシートが通ったよ。
My job application has been accepted.

❺ 司法試験に5回落ちちゃった。
I failed the National Bar Exam five times.

❻ テストはきっと満点だと思う。
I'm sure I got a perfect score on the exam.

❼ 面接中に一瞬、頭が真っ白になった。
I went blank for a moment during the interview.

❽ 合格者には電話で結果が通知されるんだ。
Successful applicants will be notified of their result by phone.

❾ とうとうその会社に就職が内定したよ。
At last the company unofficially decided to employ me.

❿ また、不合格通知だよ。
I got a rejection notice again.

13 会社で

I'm definitely overworked, and underpaid.

完全にこき使われて、十分な給料ももらってないよ。

Another long day of work is almost over. As soon as I've finished writing this report, I will be able to go home. I can't believe it's almost 12! I've really been burning the midnight oil this past week. Maybe once this project is finished, I'll be able to go home earlier. Oh, who am I kidding? This has been my working schedule for the last year and a half. I'm definitely overworked, and underpaid. I remember when I began working here, I was able to finish work by 6 and be home by 7. Then, my co-worker quit her job! Instead of replacing her with a new employee, my boss added her work duties to mine! Now, I have twice as much work, but my salary hasn't changed at all. It's so unfair. It's downright infuriating! I've tried to talk to Mrs. Kawamura in the Personnel Department about it, but she's always too busy to meet with me. At this rate, I'm never going to be able to have a personal life. If I were to buy a pet, it would probably die from loneliness! Ugh, no, that thought is too disgusting to contemplate! OK, I've decided. I'm going to talk to Mrs. Kawamura tomorrow, and I'm not going to take 'no' for an answer!

Key Words

- [ ] burn the midnight oil：夜遅くまで働く
- [ ] who am I kidding?：そんなことあるわけないか、なんちゃってね
- [ ] definitely：完全に
- [ ] overworked：こき使われて
- [ ] underpaid：十分な給料をもらっていない
- [ ] quit：辞める
- [ ] replace A with B：AをBと置き換える
- [ ] employee：従業員
- [ ] add A to B：BにAを加える
- [ ] downright：全く
- [ ] infuriating：腹立たしい
- [ ] at this rate：この調子だと
- [ ] disgusting：うんざり
- [ ] contemplate：じっくり考える
- [ ] not take 'no' for an answer：嫌とは言わせない

Translation

今日もまた長い1日の仕事が終わろうとしている。この報告書を書き終えたら、すぐに家に帰れる。もう12時だなんて信じられない！ 今週は本当に夜遅くまで働き通し。たぶんこのプロジェクトが終わったら、もっと早く帰れると思う。ああ、そんなことあるわけないか。1年半もの間、ずっとこんな仕事のスケジュールだし。完全にこき使われていて、十分な給料ももらってないわ。ここで働き始めた頃は、6時までには仕事を終わらせて、7時までには帰宅できたことを思い出すなあ。その後、同僚が仕事を辞めちゃったの！ 彼女と入れ替えに新しい従業員を入れる代わりに、上司は彼女の仕事を私に回したの！ 今では2倍の量の仕事をしているけれど、給料は全然変わってない。本当に理不尽だわ。全く腹立たしい！ そのことで、人事部の川村さんと話をしようとしたんだけど、彼女はいつも忙しくて会えないの。この調子じゃ、絶対にプライベートな時間を持てないわ。もし万が一ペットを買った（飼った）としても、間違いなく孤独死しちゃう。うわっダメ、そんなこと考えただけで本当にうんざりしちゃう。わかった、決心したわ。明日、川村さんと話をしよう。いやとは言わせないわ！

Point

☐ **If I were to buy a pet, it would probably die from loneliness!**
万が一ペットを買った（飼った）としても、間違いなく孤独死しちゃう！
＊ If S were to ～（動詞の原形）, S would ～（動詞の原形）｛万が一～したとしても、～だろう｝実現不可能なことを仮定する時に使うことが多い表現。

↓

★ **If the sun were to rise in the west, I wouldn't change my mind.**
万が一、太陽が西から昇っても私は考えを変えません。

Other Expressions

❶ 電車を3回乗り換えるのは面倒。
It's a pain to change trains three times.

❷ 家を出てから会社に着くまで、約1時間。
My commute is about one hour, door to door.

❸ 今夜はまっすぐ帰るか。
I think I'll go straight home tonight.

❹ 電車が遅れたから、会社に遅刻しちゃった。
My train was late, so I didn't make it to work on time.

❺ 今晩は接待の予定なんだ。
I'm entertaining clients tonight.

❻ 会社に着いて、まずすることはメールのチェック。
First of all, I check my email at the office.

❼ 今日は月曜日か。朝礼がある。
Is it Monday today? We have a morning assembly.

❽ 今日は2時から鈴木さんとの約束。
I have an appointment with Mr. Suzuki at two.

❾ 今日の会議の場所はどこかな？
Where is today's meeting going to be held?

❿ 電話が鳴ってる。出なくちゃ。
The phone is ringing. I have to answer it.

Pleasure in the job puts perfection in the work.
- Aristotle

働く喜びが大きな仕事を完璧にする。
アリストテレス

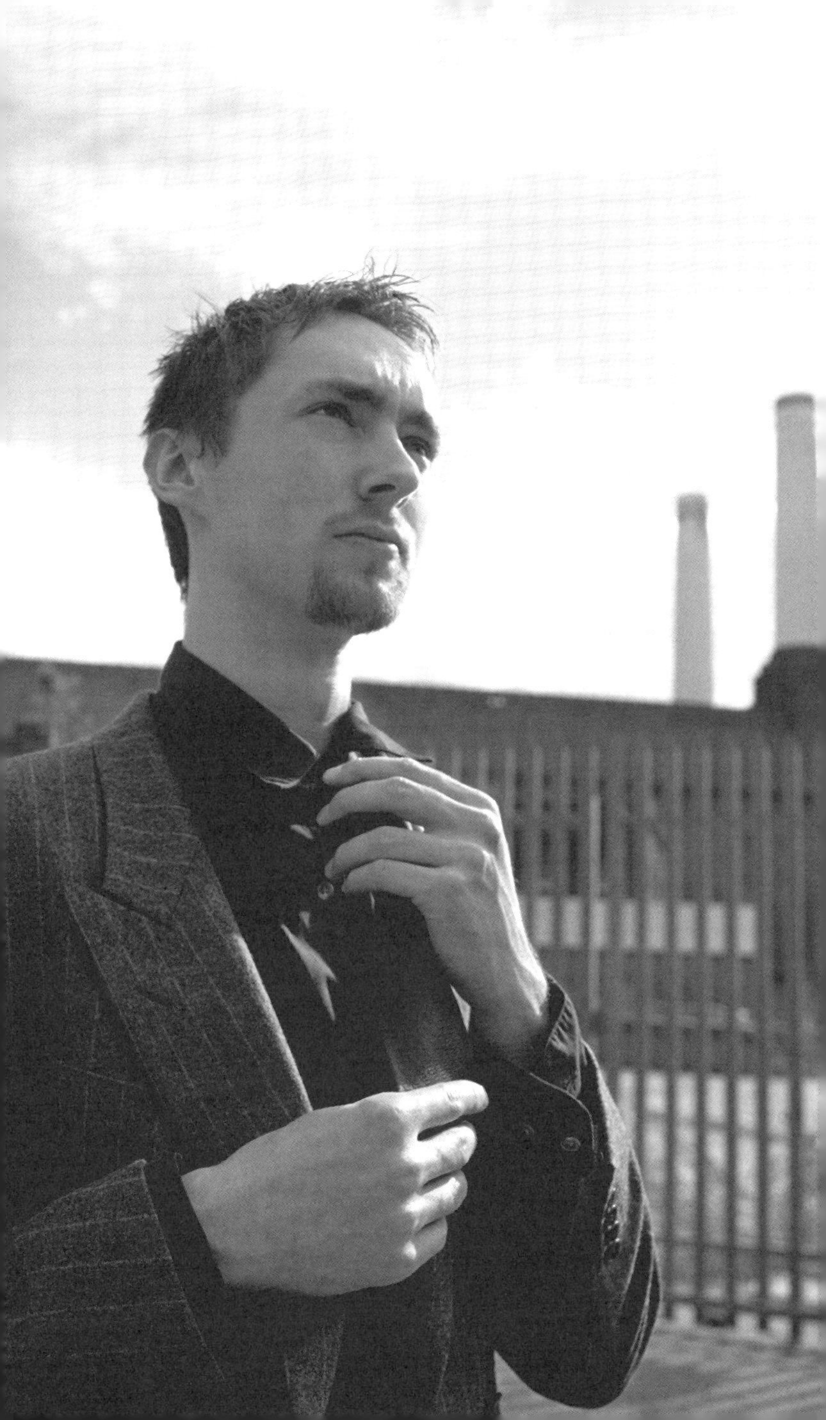

14 人事部長との交渉(1)

My work situation is so difficult.

私の労働環境はとってもつらいの。

Yes! I was able to get an appointment to meet with Mrs. Kawamura this afternoon! I need to think about how I'm going to present my case. I need Mrs. Kawamura to understand why my work situation is so difficult. I should start by talking about the positive aspects of my job! For example, the fact that I love working with computers and that I have excellent working relationships with all of the people in my department. I should also remind her that all my work evaluations have been excellent, because I take my job seriously. Oh, I should also tell her that I've never taken a sick day! And I've only taken one vacation in all the time I've been working at the company. Then, I should remind her about my co-worker in the IT Department who suddenly quit. Because of that, my workload dramatically increased. The head of the IT Department talked about replacing her, but never got around to it. Mrs. Kawamura is a really understanding person, so I think she will agree with me if I explain all of my points clearly and honestly. Well, I will cross my fingers and hope for the best!

Key Words

- appointment：(面会の)約束
- case：言い分
- aspect：側面
- relationship：関係
- evaluation：評価
- take O seriously：Oを真面目に考える
- workload：仕事量
- increase：増える
- get around to 〜：〜に至る
- agree with 〜：〜と意見が一致する
- explain：説明する
- cross one's fingers：(人差し指の上に中指を重ねて)祈る
- hope for the best：うまく行くことを祈る

Translation

そうそう。今日の午後、川村さんと会う約束を取り付けたわ。私の言い分をどうやって示したらいいかを考えなくちゃ。私の労働環境がいかにつらいものかを川村さんにわかってもらう必要があるもの。まずは、私の仕事のプラスの面を話さないとね！たとえば、コンピューターを使った仕事が大好きなことや部署の人たちとの関係もうまくいっている事実をね。自分の仕事を真剣に考えているから、仕事の評価は素晴らしいものであることも彼女に知ってもらわないと。ああ、そうそう、病気休暇を一度も取ったことがないことも言っておかないとね。しかも、会社に勤めてからたったの1度しか休暇を取っていないことも。それから、急に辞めちゃったＩＴ部の同僚のことも知ってもらわなくちゃ。お蔭で、私の仕事量が劇的に増えたことを。ＩＴ部長は代替のことを話していたけど、全くそれに至っていないしね。川村さんはすごく物わかりの良い人だから、言いたいことをハッキリと正直に全部説明すれば私の言うことを認めてくれると思う。まあ、(人差し指の上に中指を重ねて)うまく行くように祈りましょう。

Point

☐ **I need Mrs. Kawamura to understand why my work situation is so difficult.**
私の労働環境がいかにつらいものであるかを川村さんにわかってもらう必要がある。
＊need O to ～（動詞の原形）｛O に～してもらう必要がある｝

⬇

★ **I need you to tell me the news.**
君にそのニュースを知らせてもらう必要がある。

Other Expressions

❶ プレゼンまで時間があまりない。
There isn't much time left before the presentation.

❷ 会議室の予約をしないと。
I have to reserve a room for the meeting.

❸ 企画書を書くのに苦労するなあ。
I'm having trouble writing the project paper.

❹ この企画は是非通したいな。
I want this project to go through by all means.

❺ 今日の企画会議は取りやめになった。
Today's planning meeting has been canceled.

❻ この企画の主な狙いは何だろうか？
What's the main point of this project?

❼ 彼女の言いたいことはわかるが賛成できないなあ。
I understand what she means, but I can't agree with her.

❽ 企画の名称を決めるのに3時間かかったよ。
We spent three hours settling on the name for the project.

❾ プレゼンの結果が気になるなあ。
I'm anxious about the result of the presentation.

❿ やっと企画が通ったの。
At last they picked my project.

15 人事部長との交渉(2)

I am scheduled for a raise!

私は昇給が予定されているの!

I feel like I'm walking on air! The meeting with the Personnel Department went much better than I could have hoped! Mrs. Kawamura started the meeting by telling me how pleased she was with my work and that my boss had told her I worked well under pressure. She also explained that the reason why my co-worker hadn't been replaced was due to budget cuts in my department. To make up for it, they are going to hire an assistant to work under me. I will be able to give the assistant smaller tasks and busywork. That will give me more time to focus on more important tasks, and I'll be able to get work done much faster! When I heard about the assistant, I was overjoyed. But then Mrs. Kawamura gave me another great piece of news! Due to my performance on the job, she told me I was scheduled for a raise at the beginning of the next financial year! I left the meeting with a huge grin on my face. Everything worked out better than expected. Now, back to work! Until the new assistant starts working in our department, I still have a mountain of paperwork on my desk I have to do…

Key Words

- walk on air：有頂天になる、舞い上がる
- budget cuts：経費削減
- make up for 〜：〜を埋め合わせる
- busywork：忙しいだけで価値のない仕事
- task：仕事、課題
- overjoyed：非常に嬉しい
- raise：昇給
- financial year：会計年度
- huge：巨大な
- grin：笑顔
- work out：うまく行く
- a mountain of 〜：山のような

Translation

なにか舞い上がっている気分だわ。人事部長との面談は希望より遥かに良い結果になったの。川村さんは、面談のはじめに、私の仕事ぶりに満足していると言ってくれたし、プレッシャーの中で私が良く働いていると上司が言っていたことなども話してくれたの。同僚の代替がなかったのは、部署の予算カットによるものだとも説明してくれたわ。その埋め合わせに、アシスタントを雇って私の下で働かせてくれるみたい。アシスタントに細かいことや時間ばかりかかる仕事をやってもらえるようになる。そうすれば、もっと重要な仕事に集中する時間が増えて、仕事をずっと早く終わらせることもできるようになるの。アシスタントの話を聞いた時は、とっても嬉しかった。それから、川村さんは、もうひとつ最高のニュースをくれたの。仕事の業績のおかげで、来年度の初めから昇給になる予定だって教えてくれたの。満面の笑みで面談の場を出たわ。全てが予想以上にうまく行った。さて、仕事に戻ろう！ 新しいアシスタントが部署で仕事を始めるまで、しなくちゃいけないデスクワークが山のようにあるから。

Point

☐ **I'll be able to get work done much faster.**
仕事をずっと早く終わらせることもできるようになる。
 * get + O +〜過去分詞〔O を〜させる、してもらう〕
 * much +〜比較級〔ずっと〜〕

↓

★ **He got the curtain washed.**
彼はカーテンを洗ってもらった。

★ **He did the job much faster than I did.**
彼は私よりずっと早く仕事を終わらせた。

Other Expressions

❶ 3年ぶりに昇給したよ。
I got a raise for the first time in three years.

❷ 冬のボーナスは思っていたよりずっと少なかったなあ。
The winter bonus was much smaller than I expected.

❸ ほとんど毎日、残業だよ。
I work overtime almost every day.

❹ ここ数ヶ月、ずっと転職を考え中。
I've been thinking about changing jobs for the past few months.

❺ 給料が10％カットされたよ。
My salary was cut by 10%.

❻ 彼は一生懸命働かないと首になっちゃうかも。
He must work hard, or he will get fired.

❼ 安月給じゃマイホームなんか買えないよ。
I can't get my own house on my small salary.

❽ 信じられない。営業部長に昇進したんだ。
I can't believe it. I was promoted to Sales manager.

❾ 家計をやりくりするのに苦労するなあ。
I have a hard time balancing the house budget.

❿ 今月は赤字になりそうだ。
We're going to end up in the red this month.

16 通勤電車

I hate taking the morning train!

朝の電車に乗るのはもう嫌。

The morning train is crowded, as usual. I can barely breathe because I'm being squeezed by everyone around me! I thought catching an earlier train would be a good idea, but I'm starting to regret my decision. Ever since the new assistant started working at the IT Department, I've been able to get up early. I wake up every day at 5 AM, go jogging, and eat a healthy breakfast! Usually I eat a slice of grapefruit, some *natto* with a bit of rice, and drink tea or orange juice. Yesterday night, I did some research online about organic produce. I'm going to buy some at the supermarket tonight. It's only been one week since I started my healthier lifestyle, but I've already started to notice a difference. I have much more energy, which means that I can get more work done around the office. That also means I can leave the office earlier than before. I haven't had to work overtime in a week! Ouch! Some guy just stepped on my toes as the train's doors opened. I hate taking the morning train! Hmm, maybe I could come to work by bicycle. That would be excellent exercise! That's a really good idea! I'll start doing that tomorrow!

Key Words

- as usual：いつものように
- breathe：息をする
- squeeze：押しつぶす、絞る
- regret：後悔する
- online：オンラインで
- organic produce：オーガニック製品
- notice：気づく
- work overtime：残業する
- Ouch!：痛い！

Translation

朝の電車はいつものように満員。周りの人たちに押し潰されて息もできないくらい！　早い電車に乗るのは良いアイデアだけれど、自分で決めたことを後悔し始めているの。新しいアシスタントがIT部で働き始めてから、早く起きられるようになったわ。毎日、午前5時に起きて、ジョギングをし、健康的な朝食を取る。普段は、グレープフルーツを一切れと、少なめのごはんに納豆を食べ、紅茶かオレンジジュースを飲む。夕べはオーガニック製品について、ネットでちょっと調べてみたのよね。今夜、スーパーでいくつか買う予定。健康的な生活を始めてから、まだたったの1週間しか経っていないけれど、もう違いを感じ始めているの。以前よりもずっと元気になったから、会社での仕事ができるようになってきたの。つまり、前よりも早く会社を出られるようにもなったということ。この1週間、残業もしなくて済んでいる。いたっ！　電車のドアが開いた時に、どこかの男が私のつま先を踏んだわ。朝の電車に乗るのは、もう嫌。う〜ん！　自転車で通勤できるかも。そっちの方が立派な運動にもなるし。本当にいいアイデアだわ。明日から始めようっと。

Point

☐ I'm being squeezed by everyone around me.
周りの人たちに押し潰されている。
＊ be 動詞＋ being ＋〜過去分詞〔〜されている〕進行形の受動態

↓

★ A new factory is being built near the city hall.
新しい工場が市役所の近くに建てられている。

Other Expressions

❶ あっ、寝坊しちゃったよ。
   Oh, I've overslept!

❷ ひどい二日酔いだ。病気で休むって電話しよう。
   I have a terrible hangover. I'll call in sick.

❸ 何か忘れているような気がするんだ。
   I feel like I forgot something.

❹ 定期券を家に置いてきちゃった。家に戻らなくちゃ。
   I left my commuter pass at home. I have to go back home.

❺ この車両はいつもすし詰め状態。
   This car is always packed like a can of sardines.

❻ この車両の冷房、強すぎるよ。
   The air-conditioning in this car is too strong.

❼ 足を踏まないでよ。
   Don't step on my toe.

❽ 満員電車で足を組んで座るなよ。
   Don't sit with your legs crossed in the crowded train.

❾ ハンドバッグをドアに挟まれちゃった。
   I got my handbag caught in the door.

❿ 危うく乗り損なうところだったわ。
   I barely missed the train.

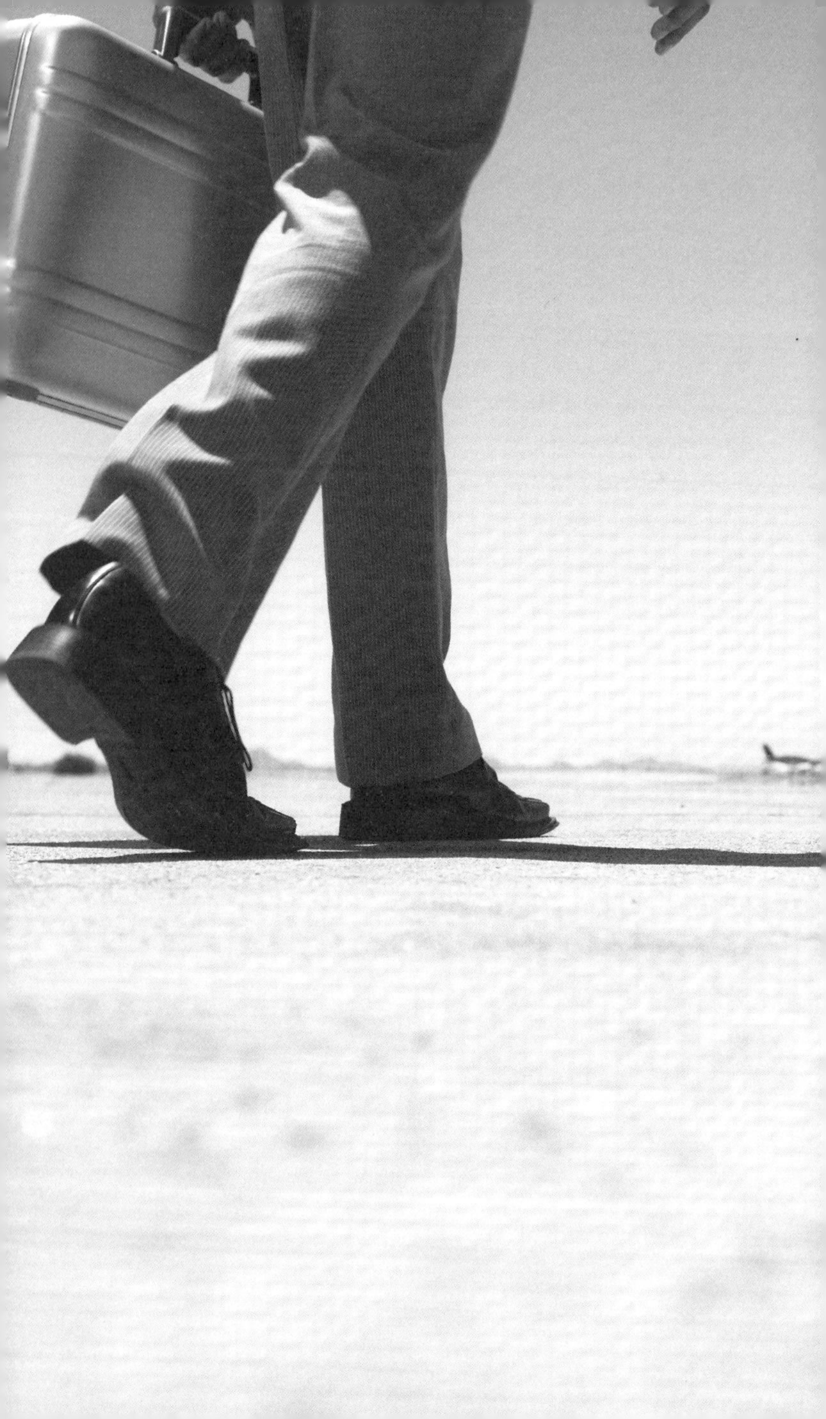

I can accept failure, everyone fails at something. But I can't accept not trying.

— Michael Jordan

失敗は受け入れられる。
誰もが失敗するから。
でも、挑戦しないでいることは
受け入れられない。

マイケル・ジョーダン

17 会社の飲み会にて

Our discussion turned into an argument.

話し合いは言い合いになっていった。

I have a splitting headache this morning! Last night, Mrs. Kawamura took me and some co-workers out for dinner, and I had too much to drink. At the end of the drinking party, I was very drunk. I still feel hung over. I can't hold my alcohol. However, Mrs. Kawamura belted down one drink after another! I never knew what a strong drinker she was. While we drank, Mrs. Kawamura asked us questions about our careers. She wanted to know what our goals were and how we planned to accomplish them. I was too drunk to answer, so Mrs. Kawamura got angry! She accused me of not thinking seriously about the future. When she said that, I became upset. I told her that I wanted to work overseas someday, and that I was the hardest-working person in my department! In the end, our discussion turned into an argument. Now, I'm really embarrassed about having been so rude to my superior. If I run into her today, it will be really awkward! I think I'll hide in my office today…

Key Words

- a splitting headache：頭が割れるような頭痛
- co-worker：同僚
- be(feel) hung over：二日酔いである
- one...after another：次から次へと…
- belt down：がぶ飲みする
- career：職業、仕事
- accomplish：達成する
- accuse A of B：BのことでAを責める
- become upset：腹が立つ
- overseas：海外で
- in the end：結局
- turn into 〜：〜になる
- argument：口論、言い合い
- embarrassed：きまりが悪い
- rude：無礼な、失礼な
- superior：先輩、上司
- awkward：気まずい

Translation

今朝は頭が割れるように痛いなぁ。夕べ、僕と同僚の数名が川村さんに連れられて夕食に行ったけど、飲み過ぎてしまったんだ。飲み会の終わり頃にはすごく酔っ払っていたよ。二日酔いなんだ。僕はお酒に強くない。でも、川村さんは次から次へとガブガブ飲んでいた！　彼女があんなにお酒に強いなんて知らなかったぞ。飲んでいる間、川村さんは僕たちに仕事についていくつか質問をした。僕たちの目標がどんなもので、それをどうやって達成するつもりかを知りたがっていたんだ。僕は酔っていて答えられなかったから、川村さんは腹を立ててしまった。彼女は将来のことを真剣に考えていないと言って僕を責めた。彼女がそう言った時、僕は腹が立った。いつか外国で働きたいこと、部署では僕が一番の働き者だということを彼女に言った。結局、話し合いは言い合いになってしまった。今になってみると、先輩に対してあんなに無礼に振る舞ってしまって本当に決まりが悪い。もし今日、彼女に出くわしたら、本当に気まずいな。今日は、会社の中で隠れていよう！

Point

☐ **I have a splitting headache this morning!**
今朝は頭が割れるように痛い！
* have a〜（形容詞）headache〔〜な頭痛がする〕

↓

★ **a slight headache**：軽い頭痛
★ **a bad headache**：ひどい頭痛
★ **a throbbing headache**：がんがんする頭痛

Other Expressions

❶ 接待も仕事のうち。
   Entertaining clients is part of the job.

❷ 乾杯の音頭を取るのは誰かな？
   Who is going to give an initial toast?

❸ 上司にお酒をつがないと。
   I have to pour a glass for the boss.

❹ 接待されるのは今回が初めて。
   This is the first time I've been wined and dined.

❺ ビールで乾杯しよう。
   Let's start off with some beer.

❻ 彼はお酒が強そう。
   It seems he can hold his alcohol well.

❼ お酒が回ってきた。
   The alcohol is going to my head.

❽ ちょっと酔いを覚ました方がいいよ。
   I think you'd better sober up a little.

❾ 二次会は行きたくないなあ。
   I don't want to go to the second party.

❿ パーティーは盛り上がって来た。
   The party is getting into full swing.

18 転勤の辞令を拝受

I will be transferred to our company's New York branch!

自社のニューヨーク支店に転勤になるんだ!

I received some unexpected news at work today. Mrs. Kawamura called me to her office for a meeting. At first, I was worried she was upset about the incident at the drinking party the other night and wanted to reprimand me. Instead, she congratulated me and told me I have been promoted and will be transferred to our company's New York branch! When I heard that, I was speechless. I've always wanted to travel abroad, and I have been hoping for a promotion for a long time. However, I never expected to be transferred so quickly! I will have to start studying English much more seriously from now on. I will also have to buy suitcases and get an overseas work visa. My biggest worry, though, is my girlfriend Karen. What am I going to tell her? She will be very upset when she finds out I'm leaving the country. She may even start crying! The time has come for me to seriously start thinking about my future with her. Long-distance relationships are very difficult to maintain, and I know I would be very unhappy living far away from her. I've got to think deeply about this.

Key Words

- incident：出来事
- reprimand：叱責する
- congratulate：祝う
- promote：昇進させる
- transfer：転勤させる
- branch：支店、支社
- speechless：驚きで言葉もでない
- from now on：今後は、これからは
- long-distance relationship：遠距離恋愛
- maintain：維持する

Translation

今日、仕事中に思いがけない知らせを受けた。川村さんの事務所に呼ばれて面談したんだ。最初、先日の飲み会でのことを怒って、叱ろうとしているんじゃないかと心配したけれど、そうじゃなく、僕におめでとうと言いながら伝えてくれた。昇進してニューヨーク支店に転勤になったって。それを聞いた時は言葉が出なかった。以前から海外には行きたいと思っていたし、長い間、昇進も望んでいたからね。でも、そんなに急な転勤は予想していなかったなあ。これからは、もっと真剣に英語の勉強を始めないと！　スーツケースも買わなくちゃいけないし、海外就労ビザも取らなくちゃならない。でも、一番の悩みはガールフレンドのカレン。彼女には何て言ったらいいだろう。僕が日本を出るって知ったら取り乱すだろうな。泣き出してしまうかもしれない。彼女との将来を真剣に考える時が来たんだ。遠距離恋愛は続けるのはとても難しいし、遠く離れて暮らすのはとっても寂しいとわかっている。じっくり考えないと。

Point

☐ **The time has come for me to seriously start thinking about my future with her.**
彼女との将来を真剣に考える時が来た。
＊ The time has come for me to 〜（動詞の原形）〔私が〜する時が来た〕

↓

★ **The time has come for me to propose to her.**
彼女にプロポーズする時が来た。

Other Expressions

❶ 私を北海道の支店に転勤させると上司から言われた。
My boss told me she was transferring me to the company's Hokkaido branch.

❷ もっと真剣に仕事に取り組むべきよ。
You should take your job more seriously!

❸ 大学に入った時から真剣に将来のことを考えるべきよ！
You should seriously start thinking about your future from the time you're in college.

❹ 英語を流ちょうに話せなければ海外勤務はホントに面倒。
Being transferred overseas can be a real hassle if you're not a fluent English speaker.

❺ 昇進のために最善を尽くしてやっているから、1ヶ月のノルマは超えているよ。
I'm doing my best for promotion, so I'm exceeding my monthly sales quotas.

❻ 海外就労ビザを取る手続きは複雑。
The procedure for getting an overseas work visa is complicated.

❼ 私は仕事に血と汗と涙を注いできた。
I've put my blood, sweat, and tears into my job.

❽ 彼はまじめに働いてないから絶対に彼が望む地位には昇進できない。
He's not a serious worker, so he'll never get promoted to the position he wants.

❾ 外国に引っ越すと母に言ったら大声で怒鳴り出した。
My mother started bawling when I told her I was moving to another country.

❿ 精を出して一生懸命働いた方がいいよ。上司が見てるから！
You'd better knuckle down and work hard. The boss is watching!

第3章 日常生活

Life

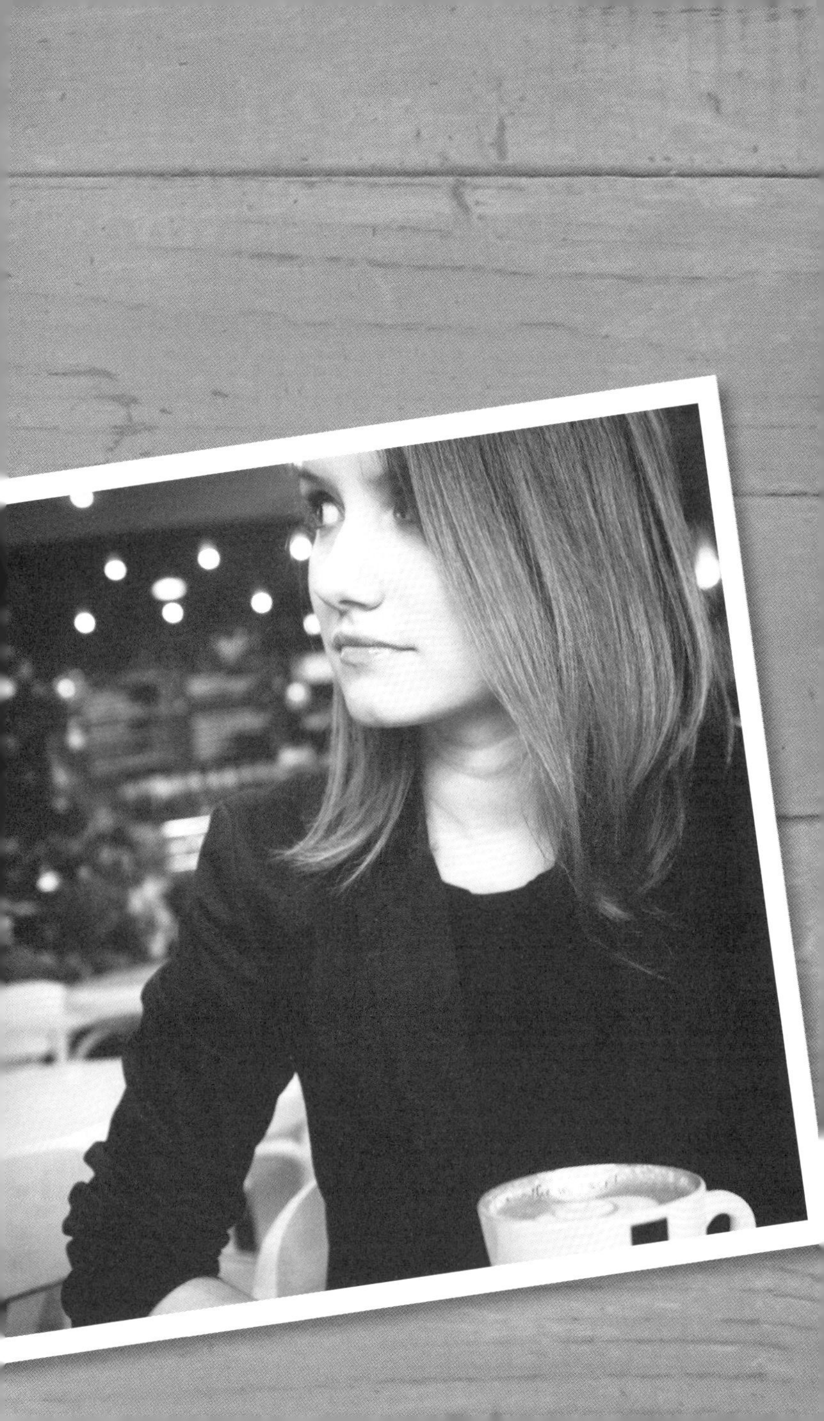

19 レストランで

I've decided to treat her to a nice meal.
美味しい食事を彼女にごちそうすることに決めたよ。

I've been thinking about how to break the news about my overseas transfer to my girlfriend. I've decided to treat her to a nice meal at an expensive restaurant. A delicious dinner will soften the blow when I tell her that I have to leave Japan in a few months. I should find the most elegant, expensive restaurant I can afford! I was thinking of taking Karen to a French restaurant, but she's actually not a big fan of French cuisine. She says that escargot is disgusting and she can't stand the taste of foie gras. Maybe an Italian restaurant would be better? But Italian restaurants usually have dishes made with cheese or milk and Karen is allergic to dairy products. It would be terrible if she had an allergic reaction! Or she could get the runs from eating too much cheese. I suppose we'll have to go to a Japanese restaurant. Karen loves sushi, so I'll find a restaurant that specializes in seafood. I heard about an elegant sushi restaurant in Ginza. It will probably cost me a lot of money, but I'm sure Karen will be happy to be treated to a delicious seafood dinner.

Key Words

- overseas transfer：海外転勤
- treat A to B：AにBをごちそうする
- blow：打撃、ショック
- afford：余裕のある
- escargot：エスカルゴ
- foie gras：フォアグラ
- allergic：アレルギーの
- dairy product：乳製品
- get the runs：下痢を起こす
- specialize in 〜：〜を専門にする

Translation

ガールフレンドに海外勤務の知らせをどう打ち明けようか、ずっと考えている途中だけれど、高級レストランで美味しい食事を彼女にごちそうすることに決めた。数ヶ月後に僕が日本を去らなければならないことを彼女に言った時のショックを、美味しい食事が和らげてくれるだろう。余裕の持てる範囲内で一番格調高い高級レストランを見つけた方がいいだろう。カレンをフレンチに連れて行こうかと思っていたけど、実際、彼女はフランス料理の熱烈なファンではない。エスカルゴは嫌いだし、フォアグラの味は耐えられないと言っているしね。たぶん、イタリアンの方が良いかな。でも、イタリアンはチーズと牛乳でできた料理が普通で、カレンは乳製品アレルギー。アレルギー反応でも起こしたら大変だ。あるいは、チーズの食べ過ぎで下痢を起こしてしまうかもしれない。和食のレストランにしよう。カレンは寿司が好きだから海鮮料理専門のレストランを探そう。銀座に格調ある寿司屋があるって聞いたことがあるなあ。相当な値段だろうけれど、カレンは美味しい海鮮料理をごちそうされれば、きっと喜んでくれるだろう。

Point

☐ I've decided to treat her to a nice meal at an expensive restaurant.
高級レストランで美味しい食事を彼女にごちそうすると決めた。
＊ I've decided to ～（動詞の原形）〔～することに決めた〕

↓

★ I've decided to open a French restaurant in Roppongi.
六本木にフレンチレストランをオープンすることに決めた。

Other Expressions

❶ ここはなかなか良いレストランだなあ。
This is a pretty good restaurant.

❷ シェフのお薦めは何だろう？
What is the chef's recommendation?

❸ このレストランはいつもいっぱいで入れない。
This restaurant is always so crowded we can't get in.

❹ 待ち時間はどれくらいかな？
How long is the wait?

❺ 予約しておけばよかった。
I should have reserved a seat.

❻ セットメニューがたくさんあって、どれを選んだらいいのか決められないや。
They have so many different combo specials that I can't decide which to choose.

❼ この店は何でもおいしいなあ。
Every dish here is delicious.

❽ ここのレストランの味、ちょっと落ちたなあ。
The food in this restaurant isn't as good as it used to be.

❾ 卵アレルギーなの。
I'm allergic to eggs.

❿ 今日のスペシャルにするかな。
I think I'll have today's special.

20 カフェで

I recommend that you check out Café Azul!

カフェ・アズルを検討してみることをお勧めします！

Last Friday, I went to a new coffee shop in downtown Tokyo. It was recommended to me by a friend of mine who's a health nut. The coffee shop is called Café Azul, and it specializes in organic coffee, tea, and other wholesome foods. The coffee beans are imported directly from a farm in the Andes Mountains in Bolivia. The beans are grown using all-natural, environmentally safe farming methods with no pesticides. The coffee has a smooth, strong taste. I consider myself a coffee gourmet, and Café Azul's espresso is the best I've ever had! I bought a bag of their coffee beans so that I could make coffee at home, too. The shop also had all-natural organic snacks and sweets, such as whole-grain muffins. They even sell goat cheeses made from the milk of mountain goats that live in the Andes! The shop's atmosphere is wonderful, with delightful rustic decorations and large posters of South America covering the walls. The only bad point is that everything is a bit more expensive than at a regular coffee shop. If money is no object, I recommend that you check out Café Azul the next time you're downtown!

Key Words

- recommend：勧める
- health nut：健康マニア
- wholesome：健康に良い
- import：輸入する
- environmentally：環境的に
- pesticide：殺虫剤
- smooth：口当たりのいい
- consider：思う
- whole-grain：全粒の
- atmosphere：雰囲気
- delightful：楽しい
- rustic：田舎の
- the next time SV：次に〜するとき

Translation

先週の金曜日、東京の繁華街にある新しい喫茶店に行って来たわ。健康マニアの友人に勧められたの。その喫茶店はカフェ・アズルという名前で、オーガニックのコーヒーと紅茶、その他の健康食品の専門店。コーヒー豆はボリビアのアンデス山脈にある農場から直輸入されたもの。豆は全て天然で、殺虫剤を使わず環境に安全な製法で栽培されているの。コーヒーの味は口当たりが良く、濃い。自分のことをコーヒーグルメだと思っているけど、カフェ・アズルのエスプレッソは、今までで一番！　家でも入れられるように、コーヒー豆を1袋買ったのよ。店には全粒のマフィンなど、100％無農薬のスナックやスイーツもあった。アンデスに生息する山羊のミルクからできたチーズも売っている。店の雰囲気はすばらしく、壁を覆う南米の田舎風の楽しい飾り付けと大きなポスターがある。ただひとつ悪いところは普通の喫茶店よりもちょっと高めなところ。お金を問題にしなければ、今度繁華街に行った時にはカフェ・アズルを検討してみることをお勧めするわ。

Point

☐ **If money is no object, I recommend that you check out Café Azul the next time you're downtown!**
お金を問題にしなければ、今度繁華街に行った時にはカフェ・アズルを検討してみることをお勧めします！
＊S is no object.〔S（時間、お金、距離など）を問わない〕主に広告で使われる表現。

↓

★ **Salary is no object.**
給料は問わない。

Other Expressions

❶ デザートに何を食べようかな？
What should I eat for dessert?

❷ ショーウインドウのチョコレートケーキ、おいしそう。
The chocolate cakes in the display window look delicious.

❸ コーヒーと紅茶のお代わり自由。
We can get free refills on tea and coffee.

❹ レモンティーがいいなあ。
I'd like tea with lemon.

❺ 紅茶にはスコーンが良く合うな。
Tea goes well with scones.

❻ いつもカフェに寄って朝食を取る。
I usually stop by a café for breakfast.

❼ コーヒーの味にはうるさいよ。
I'm particular about the taste of coffee.

❽ ケーキ付きでコーヒー一杯が500円。
A cup of coffee costs 500 yen, including a piece of cake.

❾ コーヒーはアメリカンがいい。
I want my coffee weak.

❿ 夜に濃いコーヒーを飲むと眠れなくなるよ。
Strong coffee keeps me awake at night.

21 バーで

I can't hold my alcohol.

お酒は強くないんだ。

I used to have a problem. Every time I went out drinking with my old college buddies, I ended up getting really drunk. I can't hold my alcohol, so I tried to order oolong tea instead of a drink. However, my buddies would complain that I was being a killjoy by avoiding alcohol. I was always too weak-willed to say 'no', so I ended up drinking a lot. Therefore, I've had to come up with some 'secret techniques' to avoid drinking too much when I go out with my friends. For example, I always avoid drinking beer. My friends love to compete by trying to chug beer as fast as possible. If they see me drinking beer, they pressure me into joining their drinking games! Instead, I stick to cocktails. I usually order a gin and tonic with a twist of lemon. I love the dry taste of gin mixed with soda water. I only take a few sips of my drink while my friends drink like fish. At the end of the night, my buddies usually stagger out of the bar, but I'm still fairly sober. What do you think of my 'secret technique'? It's clever, isn't it?

Key Words

- buddy：仲間
- complain：不平を言う
- killjoy：興をそぐ人
- weak-willed：意志の弱い
- therefore：だから、従って
- come up with 〜：〜を思いつく
- compete：競争する
- chug：一気に飲む
- stick to 〜：〜にこだわる
- twist：レモンなどの一片
- sip：ちびちび飲むこと
- drink like fish：大酒を飲む
- stagger：千鳥足で歩く
- fairly：かなり
- sober：しらふの

Translation

昔、困ったことがあったなあ。大学の仲間たちと飲みに出かけるたびに、いつも酔っぱらってしまっていたんだ。酒は強くないので、酒の代わりにウーロン茶を注文しようとした。だけど、仲間たちは、僕が酒を避けてその場の興をそいでいると文句を言っていた。僕は意志が弱いから、いつも嫌だとは言えず、たくさん飲んでしまっていたんだ。だから、友だちと飲みに行く時に、たくさん飲むのを避ける秘密の技を考え出したんだ。例えば、常にビールは避けること。できるだけ早く一気飲みしようと競争をするのが大好きな友だち。僕がビールを飲んでいるのを見るとゲームに加わるようプレッシャーをかけてくる。代わりに、僕はカクテルにこだわる。いつも、ひねったレモンを入れたジントニックを注文するんだ。炭酸水と混じったジンの辛い味が大好きなんだ。友だちが浴びるように酒を飲んでいる間、僕は飲み物をちびちびやるだけ。帰る頃になると、仲間たちはいつも千鳥足でバーを出るけれど、僕はまだかなりしらふ。僕の秘密の技をどう思う？　賢いでしょう？

Point

☐ **Every time I went out drinking with my old college buddies, I ended up getting really drunk.**
大学の仲間たちと飲みに出かけるたびに、いつも酔っぱらってしまっていた。
＊ every time SV 〜［〜するたびに、〜する時はいつでも］＝ whenever SV 〜

⬇

★ **Every time I see her, she is smiling.**
彼女を見るといつも微笑んでいる。

Other Expressions

❶ このバーは何時までやってるのかな？
How late is this bar open?

❷ バーは夜通し営業している。
The bar is open all night long.

❸ 今夜は何を飲もうかな。そうだなあ、いつものにするか。
What shall I drink tonight? Well, I think I'll have my usual.

❹ 私の好きな飲み物はジントニック。
My favorite drink is a gin and tonic.

❺ 20代の時はビールしか飲まなかったけど、最近はワインの味がわかるようになった。
I used to drink beer only in my twenties, but these days I came to appreciate wine.

❻ 高校時代の友だちがこのバーを経営している。
One of my friends from high school runs this bar.

❼ 昔、このバーでバーテンをやっていたの。
I used to work as a bartender in this bar.

❽ そろそろお開きにするかな。
I think it's about time to call it a night.

❾ 終電に間に合うかな？
Will I be able to catch the last train?

❿ ああ、終電に乗り損なった。タクシーに乗らなくちゃ。
Oh, I missed the last train. I have to take a taxi.

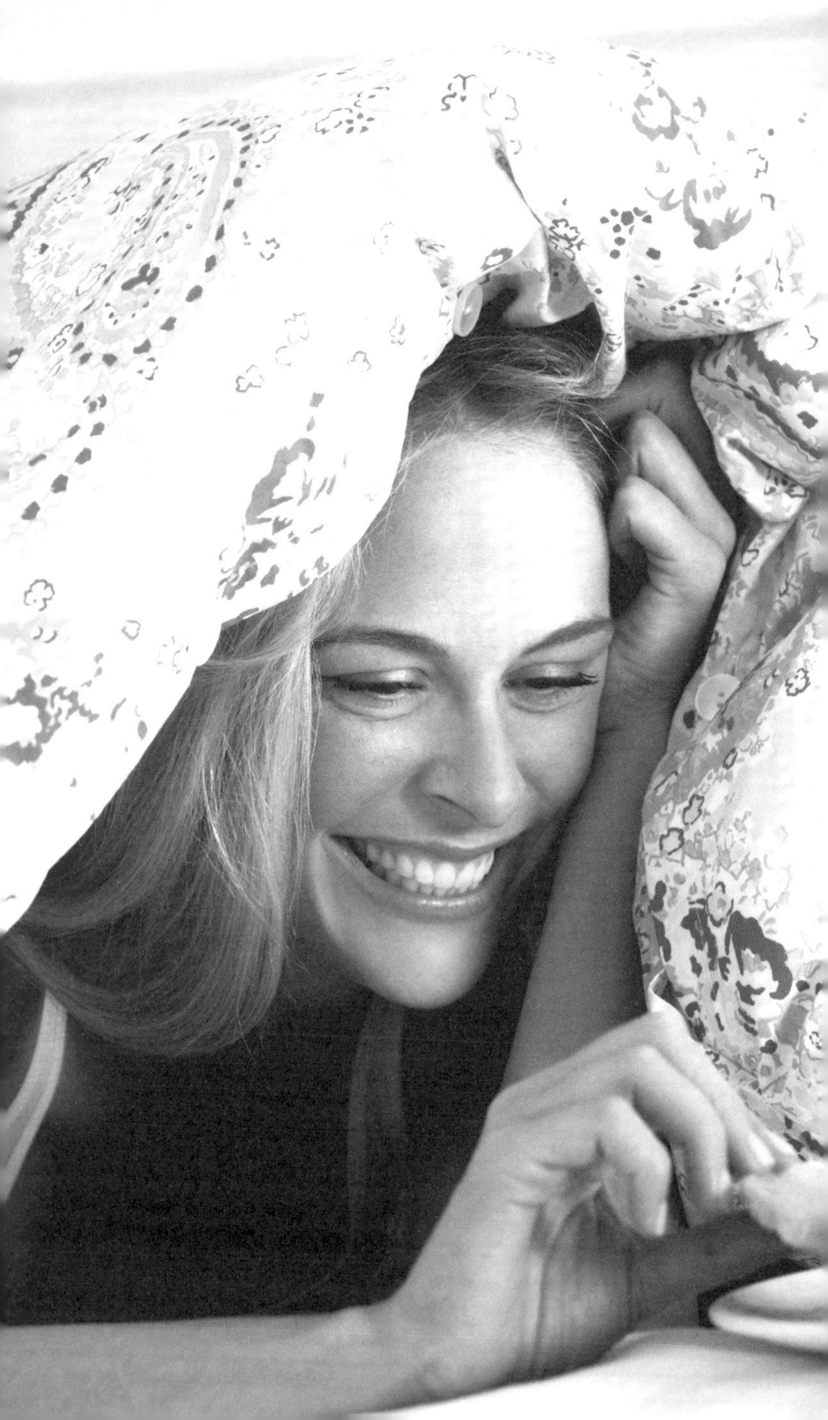

**The most important thing
is to enjoy your life
– to be happy –
it's all that matters.**
- Audrey Hepburn

一番大切なこと、それは人生を楽しむこと。
大事なのは幸せであること、ただそれだけ。
オードリー・ヘップバーン

22 喫煙室で

I felt terrible when I couldn't get my daily nicotine fix.

毎日、ニコチンを取れないと気分は最悪だったんだ。

As a former smoker, I try to avoid going into smoking areas in restaurants as much as possible. Even if there aren't any tables available in the non-smoking areas of a restaurant, I prefer waiting in the lobby instead of sitting in the smoking section. Many of my friends assume it's because the scent of tobacco would make me start craving cigarettes again, but that's wrong. Actually, since I stopped smoking, I really hate the smell of tobacco. I've heard that this is a common feeling among ex-smokers. I was a pretty heavy smoker a few years ago. I smoked a pack a day, and I felt terrible when I couldn't get my daily nicotine fix. It was my girlfriend who finally convinced me to quit smoking. She told me about all the health risks and dangers involved with smoking. She nagged me every day. I finally decided to quit just so she would stop pestering. Now, I realize how worried she was about my health. Her father used to smoke and he became very sick because of his bad habit, and she didn't want the same thing to happen to me. I'm glad she cares so much about me, so I'm never going to pick up the smoking habit again.

Key Words

- former：前の、かつての
- available：手に入る、空いている
- assume：思う
- scent：芳香
- crave：切望する
- actually：実際、実は
- ex-smoker：昔タバコを吸っていた人
- fix：一服
- convince：説得させる
- involved with ～：～に関わって
- nag：がみがみ言う
- pester：悩ます
- realize：悟る、理解する
- care about ～：～を心配する

Translation

かつての喫煙者として、レストランの喫煙席に入るのはできるだけ避けるようにしているんだ。仮にレストランの禁煙席が空いていなくても、喫煙席に座らずにロビーで待つ方を選んでいる。タバコの臭いを嗅ぐと、またタバコが欲しくなるからだと、友だちの多くは思っているけど、そうじゃない。実際、禁煙してから、タバコの臭いが本当に嫌いになったんだ。かつて喫煙者だった人たちが共通して感じていることだと聞いたことがある。僕は、数年前かなりのヘビースモーカーだった。1日に1箱吸っていたし、毎日、ニコチンを取れないと気分は最悪。最終的に、僕に禁煙するよう説得してくれたのはガールフレンド。喫煙に関する健康上の危険はすべて彼女から聞いたんだ。毎日、彼女にガミガミ言われた。とうとう禁煙することに決めたので、彼女はうるさく言わなくなった。今となっては、彼女が僕の健康のことを、いかに心配してくれていたかがよくわかった。彼女の父親は昔、タバコを吸っていて、その悪習慣から重い病気になったから、同じことが僕に起きないようにと望んでいたんだ。彼女がそんなに僕のことを心配してくれて嬉しい、だからもう2度と、喫煙の習慣を付けないようにするつもりなんだ。

Point

☐ It was my girlfriend who finally convinced me to quit smoking.
最終的に僕に禁煙を説得してくれたのはガールフレンド。
　＊ It was ～ who…〔…なのは～〕強調したい語句を「～」の部分に人を表す語句を入れる

↓

☐ It was not Jane but Mary who was injured in the accident.
事故で怪我をしたのはジェーンではなくメアリーだった。

Other Expressions

❶ 隣に座っている人、タバコ臭いな。
The guy sitting next to me smells of tobacco.

❷ 昔はタバコをたくさん吸ってたけど、今は吸ってない。
I used to smoke a lot, but not now.

❸ 誰かタバコ吸ってる。この辺は路上喫煙禁止。
I smell someone smoking. Smoking on the street is prohibited in this area.

❹ ここのカフェは禁煙環境。
This café is a smoke-free environment.

❺ 吸い殻をポイ捨てすんなよ。
Don't throw away your cigarette butts.

❻ 来月、タバコの値段がまた上がるみたい。
It seems the price of cigarettes will go up again next month.

❼ そろそろタバコを止める頃かな。
I think it's about time I quit smoking.

❽ 日本のタバコの値段は他の先進国と比べるとまだ安いなあ。
The price of cigarettes is still low, compared to other advanced countries.

❾ 外でタバコを吸うなら、最低でも携帯用灰皿を使えよ。
Use a portable ashtray at least if you smoke outside.

❿ 食事の後はタバコを我慢できないよ。
I can't resist smoking after a meal.

23 ショッピングモールで

The main advantages to shopping online are convenience and price.

ネットショッピングの主な利点は便利さと価格ね。

I usually go to the Riverside Shopping Center about twice a month, since it's on my way home from work. Whenever I stop by, I always check out the electronics store to see if they have any new or interesting gadgets, the bookstore so I can browse the newest releases, and the clothing stores, so I can see what's in fashion. I know that online shopping is becoming more and more popular these days, but I prefer going to a real store to clicking on a website. Of course, shopping online has its advantages. The main advantages to shopping online are convenience and price. You never have to leave your home, and you can find good discounts on certain websites. However, there are also benefits to shopping in a real store. You can try items before you buy them. You can actually see how a skirt will fit you before you decide whether to get it or not. You can compare between music players and see which one is best for you. You can even skim through a book before you decide if it's interesting enough to buy! To me, the benefits of shopping at a retail store definitely outweigh the drawbacks.

Key Words

- [ ] stop by：立ち寄る
- [ ] electronics store：電化製品売り場
- [ ] gadget：機械、道具
- [ ] browse：立ち読みする
- [ ] release：新発売の本
- [ ] in fashion：流行している
- [ ] certain：ある(特定の)
- [ ] item：商品
- [ ] skim through：拾い読みをする
- [ ] retail store：小売店
- [ ] definitely：ハッキリと
- [ ] outweigh 〜：〜に勝る
- [ ] drawback：欠点

Translation

職場からの帰り道にあるから、ひと月に2回くらいはリバーサイド・ショッピングセンターに行くの。立ち寄る時はいつも、家電売り場をチェックし、新しいものや面白いものがあるかどうか調べたり、本屋をチェックして最新作を立ち読みしたり、洋服売り場をチェックしてどんなものが流行っているかを見たりするの。最近は、ネットショッピングがますます流行っていると知っているけれど、ホームページをクリックするより実際の店に行く方が良いと思うわ。もちろん、ネットショッピングにも利点はいくつかある。ネットショッピングの主な利点は便利さと価格。1度も家を出ることなく、ホームページ上で割引された良い商品を見つけることができる。でも、実際のお店でのショッピングにも利点があるわ。買う前に商品を試すことができるし、買うか買わないかを決める前にスカートが自分にピッタリか実際に確かめることができる。音楽プレーヤーを比較して、どれが一番良いかを確かめることができること。買うに値するほど面白いかどうかを決める前に、本を拾い読みできること。私にとっては、小売店での買い物の利点の方が欠点よりも勝っていることは明らかね。

Point

☐ **Online shopping is becoming more and more popular these days.**
ネットショッピングがますます流行ってきている。
 * become more and more popular〔ますます流行ってくる〕同じ比較級を and でつなげると「ますます」の意味になる。

↓

★ **It's getting colder and colder.**
ますます寒くなってきた。

Other Expressions

❶ 午後、スーパーに行こうかな。
I think I'm going to the grocery store this afternoon.

❷ その店では20％引きのセールをやってるよ。
The store is having a 20% off sale.

❸ 今日の特売品は何かな？
What's on sale today?

❹ このTシャツ特売で安く買ったの。
I bought this T-shirt cheap at a bargain sale.

❺ そろそろ歯ブラシを買い換えようかな。
It's about time I got a new toothbrush.

❻ 今日は買う物がたくさんだ。
I have so many things to buy today.

❼ マヨネーズはまだあったかな？
Is there any mayonnaise left?

❽ 最近は野菜が高いなあ。
Vegetables are so expensive these days.

❾ 何か買い忘れてるような気がするな。
I feel like I've forgotten something.

❿ あっ、醤油を買い忘れた。
Oh, I forgot to buy soy sauce!

24 ショーウインドウの前で

Everything is blue this year!

今年は全てがブルーっていうこと！

Well, that settles it! After looking at all the display windows in the shopping center, it's very clear: Blue is the color that's 'in' this year. Most of the suits and shirts on display are different shades of blue. Blue jeans, blue suede shoes… everything is blue this year! Luckily, I look great in blue, so I'm going to update my wardrobe by buying a couple of navy blue sports jackets along with some light blue business shirts. I think I'll get a couple of neckties as well. This tie with the checked pattern looks especially nice, so I'll get two of them. I'm sure they'll make me look sharp at the office. I can't wait to see what compliments I get on my sartorial tastes. I should buy something for Karen while I'm at it. I'm sure she'd look lovely in this blue silk scarf. Let's see how much it costs…30,000 yen?! I just got sticker shock! I think I'll just get her a small hand mirror instead…

Key Words

- [ ] That settles it!：それで決まった。
- [ ] in：流行の
- [ ] shade：色合い
- [ ] update：更新する
- [ ] wardrobe：持ち衣装、ワードローブ
- [ ] a couple of ～：2・3の～
- [ ] along with ～：～と一緒に
- [ ] ～ as well：～もまた
- [ ] checked pattern：チェックの模様
- [ ] compliment：ほめ言葉
- [ ] sartorial：(男性)服の
- [ ] get sticker shock：高い値段にショックを受ける

Translation

さて、それで決まった！ ショッピングセンターのショーウインドウをすべて見て明らかなこと。それは、ブルーが今年の流行色だってこと。陳列されたスーツやシャツは様々な色合いのブルー。ブルーのジーンズ、ブルーのスエードシューズ、今年は全てがブルー！ 運良く、僕はブルーが似合うから、薄いブルーのビジネスシャツと一緒に、ネイビーブルーのスポーツジャケットを2、3着買って、ワードローブを新しくしよう。ネクタイも2、3本買おうかな。特にこのチェックのネクタイは素敵だから、2本買おう。つけて行ったら、きっと会社でスマートに見えるだろうな。僕の服の趣味にどんなほめ言葉をもらえるか待ち遠しいなあ。ついでに、カレンにも何か買ってあげた方がいいかな。このブルーのシルクのスカーフきっと似合うな。ええと、いくらかな。3万円！？ ああ、ショック！ 代わりに、彼女には小さな手鏡を買うことにしよう。

Point

☐ **I should buy something for Karen while I'm at it.**
ついでに、カレンにも何か買ってあげた方がいいかな。
∗ while I'm at it〔ついでに〕

↓

★ **I'm going for a drink. Shall I bring you one while I'm at it?**
飲み物を買いに行くけど、ついでに1つ買って来てあげようか。

Other Expressions

❶ あのショーウインドウの白いドレス素敵だわ。
That white dress in the display window is great.

❷ このスーツどうかなあ？
How do I look in this suit?

❸ このセーター似合うかなあ？
Do I look good in this sweater?

❹ 混んだ店での買い物は大嫌い。
I hate shopping in the crowded stores.

❺ 決める前に他の店を見て回るか。
I think I'll look around at some other stores before I make a decision.

❻ もう秋物が出てるんだ。
Autumn fashions are already coming out.

❼ ほしい物がありすぎてどれを買ったらいいのか決められないや。
There are so many things I want that I can't decide which one to buy.

❽ このネクタイ、青いシャツに合うかなあ？
Does this tie go well with a blue shirt?

❾ 今年の流行の色は何色かなあ？
What color is in this year?

❿ このドレスに決めたわ。
I've decided on this dress.

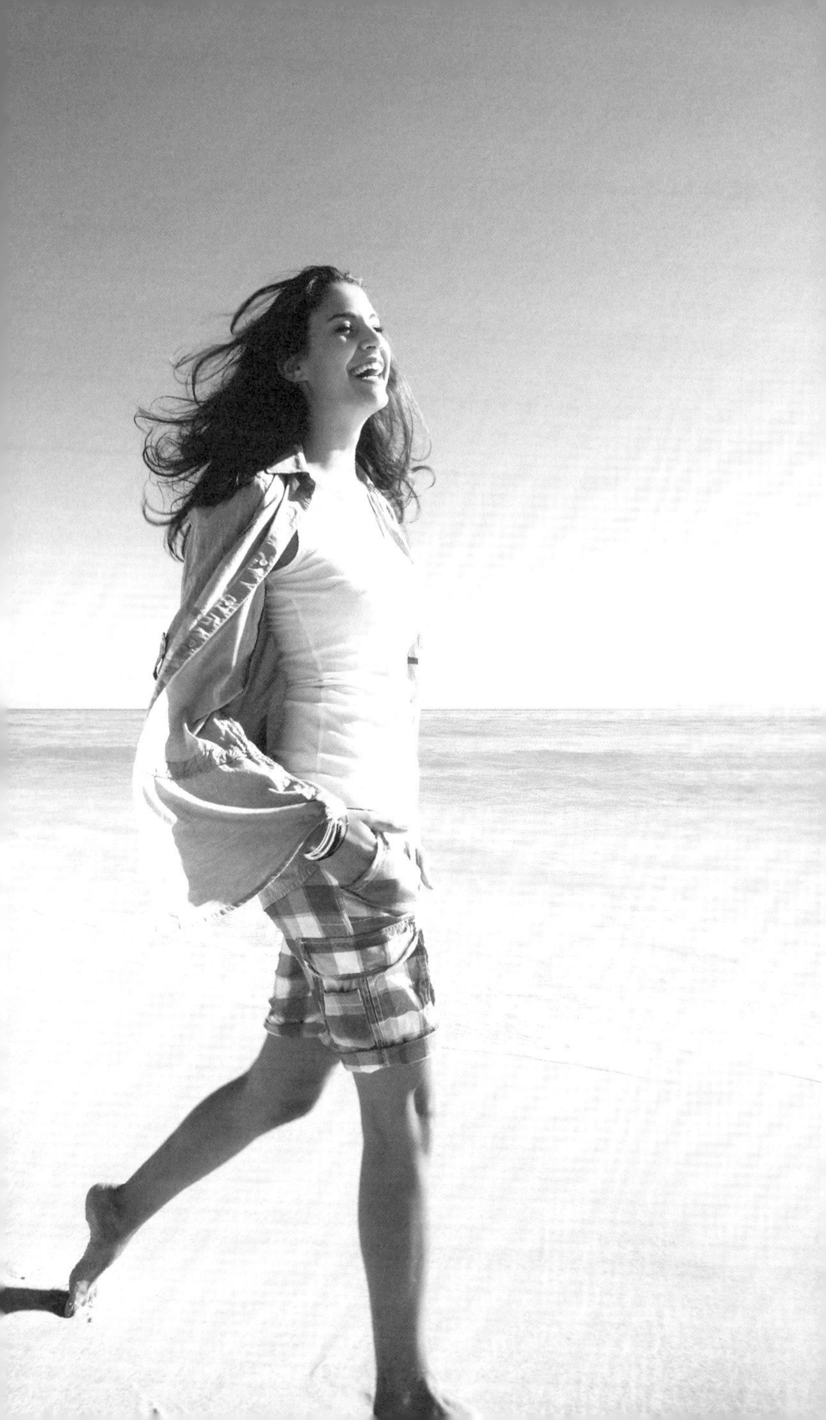

**Say you just can't live that negative way.
You know what I mean.
Make way for the positive day.
Cause it's a new day.**

— Bob Marley

ねえ、そんなマイナス思考じゃ
生きていけないよ。
わかるでしょ？
前向きに進もうよ。
だって、毎日が新しい日なんだから。

ボブ・マーリー

25 ドライブにて

She has a terrible sense of direction.

彼女はひどい方向音痴だなあ。

I've never been much of a driver. I don't even own a car! My girlfriend, on the other hand, loves driving. She says that a leisurely drive really relaxes her after a long week of work. She and I usually go for a long drive on the weekend. Sometimes we go to the beach, other times we go to the mountains, and still other times we go to popular sightseeing spots. But wherever we go, I think my girlfriend enjoys the journey more than the destination. She recently bought a new car, and she's been driving it as much as possible. The funny thing is that even though she loves driving, she has a terrible sense of direction. She always uses a GPS device, but she often gets lost! She often jokes about this and says I'm her personal navigator. Luckily, I always have a paper map handy, so that when my girlfriend inevitably gets lost, I can point her in the right direction.

Key Words

- not much of 〜：大した〜ではない
- leisurely：のんびりとした
- sightseeing spot：観光地
- journey：行程
- destination：目的地
- recently：最近
- terrible：ひどい
- sense of direction：方向感覚
- device：装置、道具
- get lost：道に迷う
- handy：手元にある
- inevitably：必ず、必然的に

Translation

僕は大して運転がうまくない。車さえ持っていないんだ。一方、ガールフレンドは運転が大好き。1週間の長時間勤務をした後は、ゆったりと運転していると本当にリラックスできると彼女は言っている。通常、僕と彼女は、週末に長距離ドライブに行く。ビーチに行くことも、山に行くこともあれば、人気の観光地に行くことだってある。でも、どこに行っても、彼女は目的地よりも行程を楽しんでいるみたい。最近、彼女は車を買って、可能な限りたくさん運転している。おかしなことに、彼女は運転が大好きなのに、ひどい方向音痴なんだ。いつもGPSを使っているけど、よく迷子になっちゃう。よく彼女はこれを笑いとばして、僕が彼女のナビだって言っている。幸い、彼女がいつも迷子になる時は、正しい方向を示してあげられるように、僕はいつも紙の地図を手元に置いてあるんだ。

Point

☐ Sometimes we go to the beach, other times we go to the mountains.

ビーチに行くことも、山に行くこともある。

＊ Sometimes SV…, (and) other times SV〜
{…することもあれば〜することもある}

↓

★ Some houses are white, and others are red.

白い家もあれば赤い家もある。

Other Expressions

❶ 交通渋滞に巻き込まれたみたい。
It looks like we got caught in a traffic jam.

❷ また迷子になっちゃった！ カーナビをつけなくちゃ。
We got lost again! I need to get a car navigation system.

❸ 道を間違えちゃったかなあ。
I might have taken the wrong road.

❹ 箱根はこの道でいいのかなあ？
Is this the right road to Hakone?

❺ 次のサービスエリアまでどれくらいかな？
How far is it to the next rest stop?

❻ 次のサービスエリアで休憩しよう。
Let's pull over at the next rest stop.

❼ 駐車場、すごく混んでる！
The parking lot is so crowded!

❽ ガソリンがなくなってきたよ。
We're running out of gas.

❾ 次のガソリンスタンドで止まらないと。
I have to pull over at the next gas station.

❿ 海の景色、きれいだなあ！
What a wonderful view of the ocean!

26 病院にて

The doctor asked me the usual questions about my health history.

医者から既往歴に関するいつもの問診を受けたよ。

I went to the hospital yesterday for my annual checkup. Since I'll be going to New York in a couple of months, I wanted to make sure I was in tip-top shape. The doctor asked me the usual questions about my health history, drew some blood, and then took my blood pressure. I was shocked when he told me my blood pressure was a bit high. I'm sure it's due to the stress of my upcoming transfer, as well as the fact that I haven't been eating well recently. I've been working late so most of my meals are sandwiches or rice balls from the local convenience store. The doctor looked at me sternly and told me I needed to make some serious changes in my diet. He also recommended I start taking a multi-vitamin supplement in the morning so that I wouldn't suffer from a vitamin deficiency. Finally, he recommended I go to a gym at least twice a week and do aerobic exercises. I'm going to take his advice seriously. I've got to start taking better care of myself!

Key Words

- annual：1年に1回の、毎年の
- checkup：健康診断
- in tip-top shape：最高のコンディションで
- health history：既往歴
- blood pressure：血圧
- upcoming：やがてやって来る
- transfer：転勤
- rice ball：おにぎり
- sternly：怖い目で
- diet：食事法
- multi-vitamin：数種のビタミン
- supplement：サプリメント
- suffer from 〜：〜に悩む
- deficiency：不足、欠乏
- aerobic exercise：有酸素運動
- take care of 〜：〜の世話をする、大事にする

Translation

昨日、年に1度の健康診断を受けるために、病院に行ってきた。数か月後にニューヨークに行くことになっているから、最高のコンディションであることを確かめたかったんだ。医者からは既往歴に関するいつもの問診を受け、採血してから血圧を測った。血圧がちょっと高めだと言われた時はショックだったな。きっと、最近は十分食事を取れていないだけでなく、間近に迫っている転勤のストレスが原因だと思う。遅くまで働いているので、食事の大半は地元のコンビニで買うサンドイッチかおにぎり。医者からは怖い目で見られ、本気になって食事を変えないとだめだって言われてしまった。また、ビタミン不足にならないように、午前中に数種のサプリメントを摂るように勧められたよ。最後に、1週間に最低2回はジムに行って、有酸素運動をするよう勧められた。本気で彼のアドバイスを受け入れようと思う。自分をもっと大事にしないとね！

Point

☐ I'm sure it's due to the stress of my upcoming transfer, as well as the fact that I haven't been eating well recently.

きっと、最近は十分食事を取っていないことだけでなく、間近に迫っている転勤のストレスが原因だと思う。
＊A as well as B〔BだけでなくAも〕

↓

★ I do the cooking as well as the washing.
私は洗濯だけでなく料理もします。

Other Expressions

❶ 明日は年に1度の健康診断。
　We have an annual checkup tomorrow.

❷ 今日の9時以降は何も食べちゃいけない。
　I'm not supposed to eat anything after 9 o'clock tonight.

❸ 今夜、お酒は控えておくか。
　I think I'll refrain from drinking tonight.

❹ バリウム、飲みたくないよ。
　I don't want to take a barium meal.

❺ バリウムと胃カメラ、どっちを選んだらいいかなあ？
　Which should I choose, a barium meal or a gastric camera?

❻ 血圧は上が160で下が90。
　My blood pressure is 160 over 90.

❼ 血圧はちょっと高めと医者から言われた。
　The doctor said my blood pressure is a bit high.

❽ データによると肝臓がやられてるらしい。
　The data shows that I have a bad liver.

❾ 運動するように医者から勧められた。
　The doctor advised me to do some exercise every day.

❿ ちょっと太り気味だからダイエットをしようと思う。
　Since I'm a bit overweight, I'm going on a diet.

第4章 趣味・価値観

Hobby

27 機内で

I'm on an airplane over the Pacific Ocean!

今、太平洋上空を飛行機で飛んでいるんだわ！

I'm going to Hawaii! I saved up some money and took five days off from work so I could take this trip, and now I'm on an airplane over the Pacific Ocean, on my way to a sunny beachside paradise! I'm going to be staying on the main island of Oahu, in a resort near Waikiki Beach. I have a very full itinerary. I want to go surfing and scuba diving at the beach. I also want to buy some foreign goods at the shopping mall. I'm interested in brand-name goods, and my friends told me they're cheaper in the US than they are in Japan. I hope there's a sale at the shopping center, so I can get some good discounts! And even though I have two left feet, I signed up for some hula dancing lessons! I'll be able to impress my friends back home with my hula dancing skills! And maybe I'll even meet a handsome foreign guy! I'm sure it's unlikely that I'll meet a guy in only five days, but I can dream, can't I?

Key Words

- [ ] save up 〜：〜を貯める
- [ ] take...days off (from work)：仕事を…日休む
- [ ] itinerary：旅程
- [ ] foreign goods：外国製品
- [ ] brand-name goods：ブランド品
- [ ] sale：特売
- [ ] have two left feet：不器用である
- [ ] impress：印象づける
- [ ] skill：技術

Translation

今、ハワイに向かっているの。この旅行のために貯金して5日間休暇を取って、今、太平洋上空の機内で、晴れたビーチサイドパラダイスに向かう途中。オワフ島のワイキキビーチ近くのリゾートに滞在する予定なの。オワフ島での旅程はびっしりと詰まっているわ。ビーチに行ってサーフィンやスキューバダイビングがしたいなあ。ショッピングモールで外国製品も買いたいわ。ブランド品に興味があるんだけど、日本よりアメリカの方が安いって友だちから聞いたの。ショッピングセンターのセールでディスカウントの商品が買えるといいなあ。私は不器用だけど、フラダンスの講習を申し込んだわ。帰ったら私の友だちにフラダンスの技術を印象づけることができる！ もしかしたら、ハンサムな外国人の男性とも出会えるかもしれないわ。まあ、たったの5日間で男性と出会うことは、きっとないと思うけど、夢見ることはできるわよね。

Point

☐ It's unlikely that I'll meet a guy in only five days.

まぁたったの5日間で男性と出会うことはないだろう。
  * It's unlikely that SV 〜 ｛〜することはないだろう｝ It's likely that SV 〜なら「〜しそうだ」の意味になる。

⬇

★ It's unlikely that Japan's economy will improve in a year.

1年で日本の景気が回復することはないだろう。

Other Expressions

❶ 運良く、窓側の席だ。
   Luckily, I had a window seat.

❷ 飛行機は予定通りに成田を離陸。
   Our plane took off from Narita on schedule.

❸ 飛行機は真夜中にシンガポールのチャンギ空港に到着。
   Our plane landed at Changi Airport in Singapore in the middle of the night.

❹ 1時間時計を遅らせないと。
   I have to set my watch back one hour.

❺ グアムに着く前に時計を1時間進めておこう。
   I'm going to set my watch ahead one hour before getting to Guam.

❻ 今どの辺を飛んでいるのかなあ？
   Where are we flying over now?

❼ 下に富士山がはっきり見える。
   I can get a clear view of Mt. Fuji below.

❽ 現地時間は何時かなあ？
   What's the local time?

❾ 東京の夜景は実にすばらしい。
   The night view of Tokyo is wonderful, indeed.

❿ シドニーの天気はどうかな？
   What is the weather like in Sydney?

28 映画館で

I managed to get tickets.

チケットを何とか手に入れたの。

Tonight is going to be really exciting. I managed to get tickets to the premiere of "The Exterminator Part 5," a new action movie starring Bruce Malone, my favorite actor. I've been watching Malone's movies since I was in junior high school. He's 65 years old, but he's still making thrilling action films filled with explosions, amazing special effects, and exciting stunts. He said in an interview that he refused to do a movie if it didn't have at least five explosions. Some people say he's over the hill, but I think he's still the coolest action star in the world. He always says catchy one-liners in all his movies. For example, in "The Exterminator Part 3," after he set the villain's home on fire with the villain still inside it, he said "Nice day for a barbecue!" That was so cool! When I heard he was actually going to appear in person tonight, my heart skipped a beat. I wonder if I'll get a chance to shake his hand, or get an autograph!

Key Words

- manage to 〜：なんとか〜する
- premiere：(公演、上映の)初日
- starring 〜：〜主演の
- explosion：爆発
- amazing：素晴らしい
- effect：効果
- stunt：スタント
- refuse：拒否する
- over the hill：最盛期をすぎて
- one-liner：短くてもユーモアに富んだセリフ
- villain：悪役
- in person：自ら、じかに
- one's heart skips a beat：心臓が止まるほど興奮する
- autograph：サイン

Translation

今夜は本当に興奮しそう。大好きな俳優のブルース・マロン主演のアクション映画、新作「エクスターミネイター5」の初日のチケットを何とか手に入れたの。中学生の頃から、マロンの映画はずっと観ているの。彼は65歳だけど、爆発や素晴らしい特殊効果、ハラハラさせるスタントが盛りだくさんのスリリングなアクション映画を作っているのよ。少なくとも5回の爆発がないと映画の出演を断る、とインタビューの中で言っていたの。もう彼は最盛期を過ぎていると言う人もいるけれど、私は、彼は今でも世界で一番かっこいいアクションスターだと思っているわ。彼は常に全作の中で、キャッチーでユーモアに富んだセリフを言っているの。たとえば、「エクスターミネイター3」では、悪役のいる家に火をつけて「絶好のバーベキュー日和」だと言っていたわ。本当にかっこよかった。今晩、彼が自ら舞台に現れると聞いた時、心臓が止まるほど興奮したの。彼と握手して、サインをもらえるチャンスがあるかしら。

Point

☐ **Tonight is going to be really exciting.**
今夜はホントわくわくしそう。
＊ be going to 〜動詞の原形 {〜しそうだ} 確かな証拠や前兆などから判断して「きっと〜になる」という断定的な推量を表す表現。

↓

★ **Look at the black clouds. It's going to rain.**
黒い雲を見て。雨が降りそう。

Other Expressions

❶ この映画館では今何をやってるのかなあ？
What's on at this movie theater?

❷ 僕はＳＦものが大好き。
I'm very fond of science-fiction movies.

❸ 最近は滅多に映画館には行かない。
I hardly ever go to the movies these days.

❹ これは今まで観た中で一番おもしろい映画だ。
This is the most exciting movie I've ever seen.

❺ その映画は思っていたほどおもしろくなかった。
The movie wasn't as exciting as I expected.

❻ とっても感動的な話だったから、ラストシーンで泣いちゃった。
It was such a moving story that I cried at the end of the story.

❼ 特殊効果がすばらしかった。
The special effects in the movie were excellent.

❽ その映画は映画館に行って観る価値ありだわ。
I think the movie is worth going to the cinema.

❾ 彼女の最新作が今、日本で上映されている。
Her latest movie is now showing in Japan.

❿ ファンたちが切符売り場で列を作っていた。
The fans were lining up at the box office ticket counters.

29 本屋で

I sometimes stop by there on the weekend to browse through their books.
週末はそこに立ち寄って立ち読みすることも時々あるわ。

There's a small mom-and-pop bookstore next door to my apartment called Sunshine Books. I sometimes stop by there on the weekend to browse through their books. Since I'm such a bookworm, whenever I drop by Sunshine Books, I always buy something. Mrs. Kurosawa, the owner of the bookstore, is also a history buff, and I can always count on her to recommend some good books to me. Recently I've been reading books about the War of the Roses in England. It's such an exciting period in European history! The war was fought to decide who would succeed the throne of England during the 15th century. I always carry a book with me when I take the train. Reading is a good distraction during a long train ride. Unfortunately, since I lose track of time when I'm reading, I sometimes miss my stop!

Key Words

- [ ] mom-and-pop：小さな自営業の
- [ ] whenever SV ～：～する時はいつも
- [ ] drop by ～：～に立ち寄る
- [ ] buff：ファン、～通
- [ ] count on ～：～に頼る、当てにする
- [ ] fought：fight（戦う）の過去分詞形
- [ ] succeed：継承する
- [ ] throne：王位
- [ ] distraction：気晴らし
- [ ] lose track of ～：～がわからなくなる
- [ ] miss one's stop：乗り過ごす

Translation

アパートの隣にサンシャインブックスという小さな自営業の本屋があるの。週末はそこに立ち寄って立ち読みすることも時々あるわ。私は本の虫だから、サンシャインブックスに寄ると、いつも何かを買ってしまうの。店主の黒澤さんも歴史通で、いつも彼女に頼って良い本を薦めてもらっているのよ。最近、イングランドのバラ戦争の本を読んでいるわ。ヨーロッパ史の中ではとっても刺激的な時代。その戦争が起こったのは15世紀、イングランドの王位を誰が継承するかを決めるためだった。電車に乗る時はいつも本を持ち歩くことにしているの。読書は長い間電車に乗っている時のいい気晴らしになるからよ。あいにく読書している時は時間がわからなくなるから、乗り過ごしてしまうことがあるの。

Point

☐ **I'm such a bookworm that whenever I drop by Sunshine Books, I always buy something.**
私って本の虫だから、サンシャインブックスに寄る時にいつも何かを買ってしまう。
* such ～（名詞）(that) SV…｛とても～だから…｝

↓

★ **I was in such a hurry that I forgot my commuter pass.**
とても急いでいたので定期券を忘れちゃった。

Other Expressions

❶ ここは古本屋がたくさんあるところとして有名。
This place is famous for its area where there are many second-hand bookshops.

❷ ここは埼玉県で一番大きな書店。
This is the biggest bookshop in Saitama.

❸ 昔、この道路沿いに小さな本屋があった。
There used to be a small bookshop along this street.

❹ ここの書店は医学書しか扱ってない。
This bookshop deals in medical books only.

❺ なんて大きな書店！ 旅行のガイドブックはどこかなあ。
What a big bookshop! I wonder where I can get a tour guide book.

❻ 暇つぶしにあの本屋に寄ろう。
Let's drop by that bookshop to kill time.

❼ たくさんの人たちが立ち読みをしている。
There are many people browsing around.

❽ 昔、学生時代に本屋でバイトをしてたことがある。
I used to work part-time at a bookshop when I was a student.

❾ 帰宅途中に駅中の書店にはよく行く。
I frequent a bookshop in the station on my way home.

❿ 来週、彼の最新作が出る。
His latest book will be released next week.

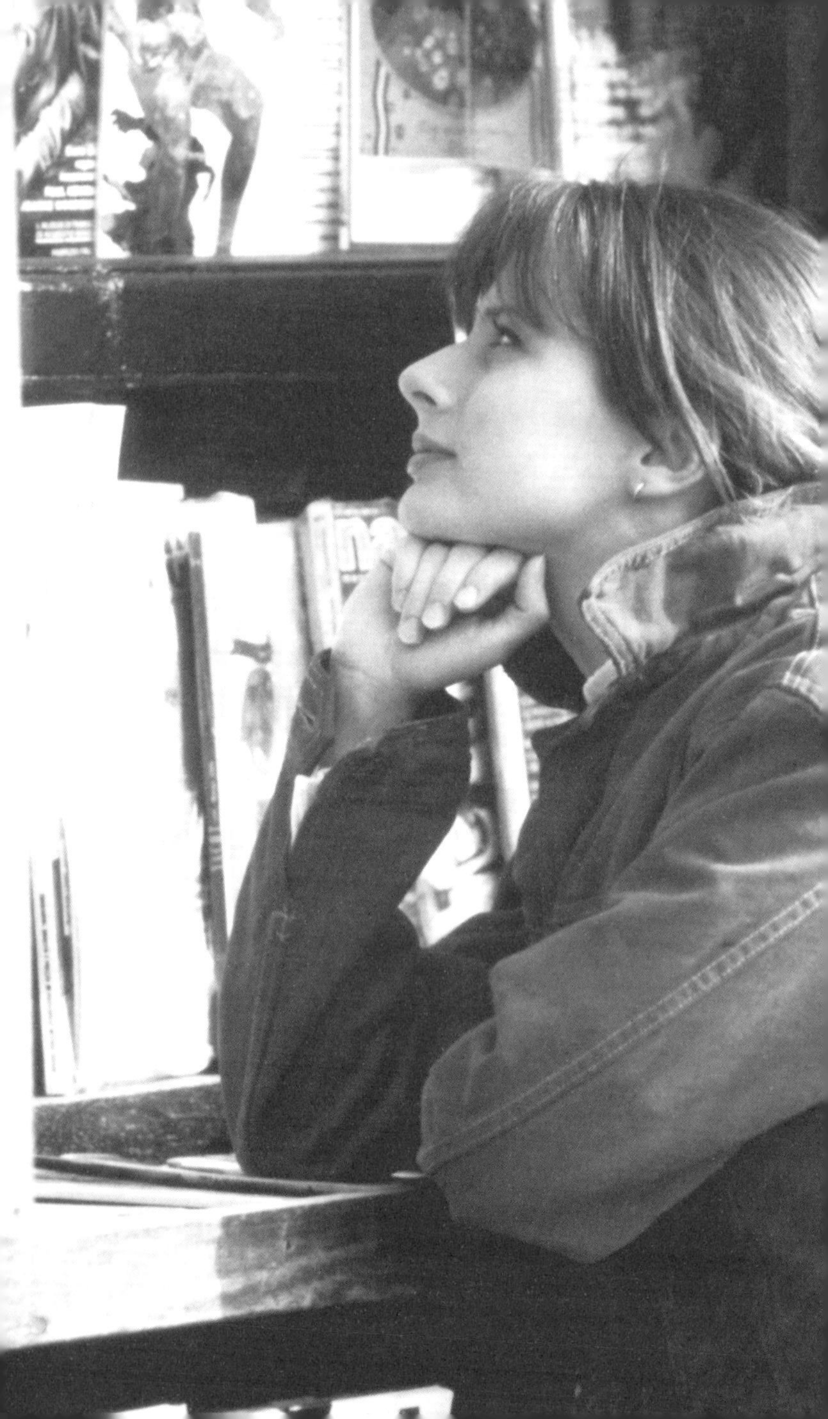

The reading of all good books is like a conversation with the finest minds of past centuries.
- Descartes

全ての良書を読むことは、
過去の最も優れた人たちと
会話をするようなものである。
デカルト

30 英会話学校で

I want to be able to speak fluently.

流暢に話せるようになりたいな。

In preparation for my trip abroad to New York, I've signed up at an English conversation school. I think it's a good idea to get some practice talking to native speakers before my big move to New York. I chose a school that's near my workplace. They have a special rate for when two people sign up for their classes – my girlfriend signed up as well, so we got a big discount! We're taking classes twice a week, practicing business English and daily conversation. I want to be able to speak fluently, so I'm taking the highest-level English course that the school offers. It can be very tricky at times, because English is so different from Japanese. I find that the best way to study is by practicing words and expressions in conversations, using them many times until I have them memorized. Once I've learned them by rote, it becomes easier to use them during casual English conversation. My girlfriend is having a much easier time of it than me – it seems languages just come naturally to her! The classes are giving me a little trouble, so I'm green with envy.

Key Words

- in preparation for 〜：〜に備えて
- sign up：(署名して)契約する
- special rate：特別料金
- fluently：流暢に
- tricky：厄介な
- at times：時々
- memorize：暗記する
- by rote：機械的に
- casual：普段の
- green with envy：羨ましい

Translation

ニューヨークへの旅に備えて、英会話学校でレッスンを受ける契約をした。ニューヨークへの大移動の前にネイティブと話す練習をするのは良い考えだと思う。職場から近い学校を選んだんだ。2人でレッスンに申し込む場合、特別料金がある。ガールフレンドも契約したので、かなり安くなったぞ。週に2回レッスンがあって、ビジネス英語と日常会話を練習している。流暢に話せるようになりたいから、学校が提供する中で一番高いレベルの英語コースを取っている。英語は日本語とかなり違うので、とても厄介なこともある。一番の勉強方法は会話の中で単語や表現を練習し、覚えるまで何度もそれらの単語や表現を使うことだと思う。いったん丸暗記してしまえば、普段の会話の中で使うのが簡単になる。ガールフレンドは僕よりもずっと覚えるのが早い。彼女には言葉がとても自然に入ってくるみたい。僕は授業にちょっと苦労しているから羨ましい。

Point

□ **The best way to study is by practicing words and expressions in conversations.**
一番の勉強方法は会話の中で単語や表現を練習すること。
＊ the best way to 〜 is by…ing ｛〜する一番の方法は…すること｝

↓

★ **The best way to get there is by taking a taxi.**
そこに行く一番の方法はタクシーに乗ること。

Other Expressions

❶ 6年間も英語を勉強してるのに、どうして話せないのかなあ？
Why can't I speak English though I have studied it for six years?

❷ 彼女のように流暢に英語を話せるようになれたらなあ。
I wish I could speak fluent English like her.

❸ 英語の本を読むことはできるけど、話すことが上手にできない。
I can read English books, but I can't speak it well.

❹ 英語の学校に行こうと思っているんだけど、どこかお薦めのところある？
I'm thinking of going to an English school. Which school would you recommend?

❺ 英会話の学校はたくさんありすぎて、どこにしたらいいかわからない。
There are so many English conversation schools that I don't know which to choose.

❻ 英語上達の一番の方法は何だろう？
What is the best way to improve my English?

❼ 英語上達の一番簡単な方法は留学することだけど、そんな余裕はない。
The easiest way to improve my English is by studying abroad, but I can't afford it.

❽ 授業は60分。ワンレッスンいくらだろう？
They have a 60-minute class. How much is each lesson?

❾ ワンレッスン3000円？ 高くない？
Three thousand yen for each lesson? Isn't that expensive?

❿ 学校に行ける余裕はないから自分で勉強するか。
Since I can't afford to go to school, I think I'll study on my own.

31 ジムで

I don't want to look like a female bodybuilder!

女性ボディービルダーみたいになりたくないわ！

Exercising in the morning is great, but there's only so much that you can do in your living room. I signed up at a local gym. I go to the gym about three or four times a week, usually at night. For my workout routine, I start by using the treadmill for twenty minutes. Then, I switch to the stationary bicycle for another twenty minutes. These are great cardiovascular exercises. They help get the body's circulation flowing. After I'm done with that, I do some simple yoga exercises using an exercise ball. I can use yoga techniques to work on my legs, my back and my stomach. I always avoid the weight room because I don't want to look like a female bodybuilder! Finally, I go home. After I go to the gym, I'm so exhausted that I pass out as soon as my head hits the pillow. The next day, my muscles always ache – but it's worth it!

Key Words

- workout：トレーニング
- treadmill：ランニングマシーン
- stationary：固定した
- cardiovascular：循環器の
- circulation：循環
- stomach：お腹
- exhausted：疲れ切った
- pass out：意識が飛ぶ
- pillow：枕
- muscle：筋肉
- ache：痛む
- worth 〜：〜に値する

Translation

朝の運動は最高だけどリビングでできることには限界があるから、地元のジムに入会申し込みをしたの。ジムに行くのは1週間に3、4回で、たいていは夜。お決まりのトレーニングとしては、20分間のランニングマシーンで始まる。それから、次の20分間はエアロバイクに移るの。これらは最高の循環器運動よ。こういう運動をすると体の血液の循環が滑らかになるの。それが終わったら、バランスボールを使った簡単なヨガね。ヨガのテクニックを使って、脚や背中やお腹の運動ができるのよ。女性ボディービルダーみたいになりなくないからウエイトルームはいつも避けているわ。ようやく帰宅。ジムに行った後は、クタクタだから横になった瞬間に、意識が飛んじゃう。翌日はいつも筋肉痛だけど、やる価値はあるわ。

Point

☐ **I'm so exhausted that I pass out as soon as my head hits the pillow.**
クタクタだから横になった瞬間に、意識が飛んじゃう。
＊ so ～（形容詞、副詞）that SV… ｛とても～なので…｝

↓

★ **He is so funny that I can't help laughing.**
彼はおもしろいから笑わずにはいられない。

Other Expressions

❶ 駅の近くのジムに入会しようか考え中。
I'm thinking about signing up for the gym near the station.

❷ まずは、縄跳びを100回やろう。
First of all, I'll jump rope a hundred times.

❸ 懸垂は1回もできない。
I can't do a single chin-up.

❹ ランニングマシーンは好きじゃないので、雨が降ってない時は外でジョギングする。
Since I don't like treadmills, I jog outside when it's not raining.

❺ ジムに行った時には20分は泳ぐようにしている。
I try to swim for at least twenty minutes when I go to the gym.

❻ ジムに通い始めてから3キロやせた。
I've lost 3 kilos since I began to go to the gym.

❼ 最近、体の調子がいい。
I've been in good shape lately.

❽ 今日はどんなトレーニングをしようかな？
What kind of workout should I do today?

❾ 今日のエアロビのクラスは何時からかなあ？
What time does today's aerobics class start?

❿ このロッカールームは広くて使いやすい。
This locker room is spacious and easy to use.

32 習い事

We spend the entire afternoon performing the tea ceremony.

ほとんど午後は茶道をして過ごしているわ。

Raising two kids while working full-time can be rather stressful, even in the best of times. Whenever I need to relax and ease my mind, I engage in traditional Japanese cultural activities. For example, some of my female neighbors started practicing the tea ceremony and invited me to join in. At first, I was a bit hesitant, as the last time I had performed the tea ceremony was during my high school days. The first time I tried making tea, I dropped the whisk onto the tatami mat and made a huge mess. Eventually, I got into the swing of things and now we meet almost every weekend to practice, drink green tea, and gossip about the folks in our neighborhood. We spend the entire afternoon performing the tea ceremony and chatting. As silly as it sounds, our weekend meetings really help me to relax after a hard week of work. I'm sure my kids appreciate not having their mom hounding them to do their homework and chores, too!

Key Words

- raise：育てる
- rather：かなり
- ease：休ませる
- engage in 〜：〜に参加する
- female：女性の
- neighbor：隣人
- hesitant：ためらう
- perform：行う
- whisk：茶せん
- mess：めちゃくちゃな状態
- eventually：最終的に
- get into the swing of things：調子をつかむ
- gossip：噂話をする
- folks：人たち
- entire：完全な
- appreciate：ありがたく思う
- hound：けしかける
- chores：雑用

Translation

フルタイムで働きながらの2人の子育ては、一番良い時でも、かなりのストレスがたまるものね。リラックスして心を休ませなければいけない時は、いつも日本の伝統的で文化的な活動をするの。たとえば、近所の女性の中には茶道の稽古を始めて私にも参加するように誘ってくれた。最後に茶道をしたのは高校時代だったから、最初はちょっとためらったわ。初めてお茶を入れてみた時に、茶せんを畳に落としてしまって、もうめちゃくちゃ。最終的には調子をつかめるようになり、今ではほとんど毎週練習に参加し、お茶を飲み、近所の人たちのうわさ話をしているわ。午後はずっとお茶をやりながらおしゃべりをして過ごすの。馬鹿らしく聞こえるけれど、きつい1週間を終えた後の週末の集まりは、本当にリラックスさせてくれる。子供たちも、宿題や雑用をやりなさいと母親にけしかけられないことを、きっとありがたく思っているわ。

Point

☐ **As silly as it sounds,**
馬鹿らしく聞こえるけど
* (As) 〜（形容詞）as SV…〔〜だけれど〕

↓

★ **Strange as it may sound, he can't speak English at all.**
奇妙に聞こえるかもしれないが、彼は英語が全然話せない。

Other Expressions

❶ 茶道をするとストレスが全部なくなる感じ。
Performing the tea ceremony melts away all my stress.

❷ お茶は熱すぎるから飲む前にフーッとさましてね。
The tea's too hot, so blow on it before you drink it.

❸ 調子がつかめてきたから、もう生け花は得意よ。
I got into the swing of things, and now I'm great at flower arranging.

❹ 茶道はホント心を癒してくれるわ。
The tea ceremony really soothes the soul.

❺ 一生懸命働いた後の一杯のお茶でホントくつろげるわ。
A cup of tea after a hard day of work really helps me unwind.

❻ 生け花の稽古をしろって妹がけしかけるのをやめてくれたらなあ。
I wish my sister would stop hounding me to take flower arrangement lessons with her.

❼ 君がいくら払ってくれても彼女の料理は食べない。
I wouldn't eat her cooking no matter how much you paid me.

❽ 茶碗に熱湯を注いだらティーバッグに浸して数分待つだけ。
Once you've poured the boiling water into the tea cup, just dip the tea bag and wait a few minutes.

❾ 畳の部屋でやらない限り、本当に茶道をしていることにはならないわ。
You're not really performing the tea ceremony right unless you do it in a tatami room.

❿ 着物にお茶をこぼしちゃったから、もう台無し！
I spilled tea on my kimono, and now it's ruined!

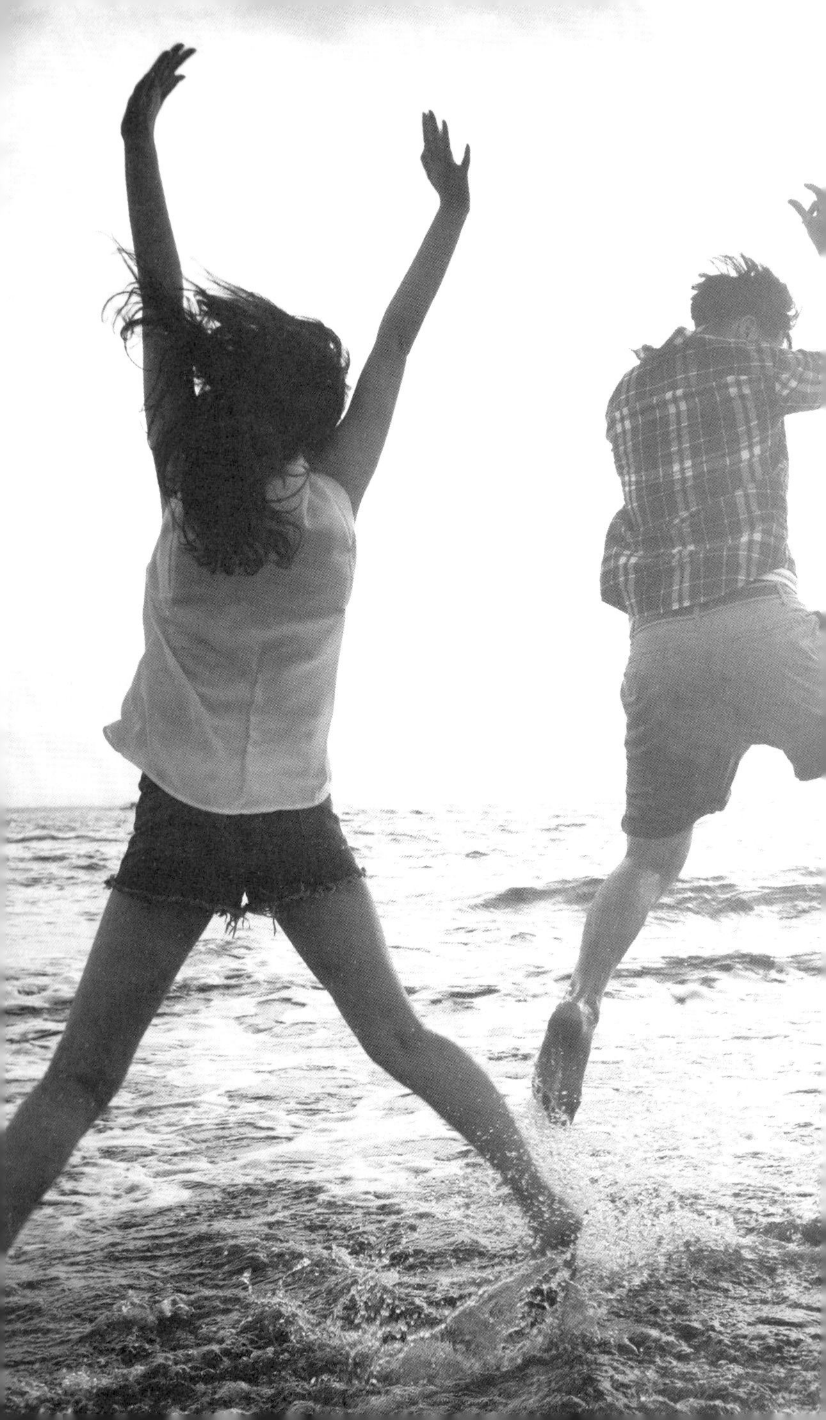

We don't stop playing because we grow old ; we grow old because we stop playing.
- Bernard Shaw

歳を取るから遊びをやめるんじゃない。
遊びをやめるから歳を取るんだ。

バーナード・ショー

33 アウトドア

My father and I used to go camping every summer.
毎年夏になると父とキャンプに行ってたなあ。

I've never liked roughing it, but I still enjoy spending time outdoors. Lately, I haven't had the time, but my father and I used to go camping every summer when I was a high school student. My dad's a pretty strong guy, and he wanted me to grow up to be strong too. That meant intensive training during the summertime. He'd take me out to the mountains for camping, and we'd stay there for a week. We'd live off the land by fishing in the nearby river and cooking by fire at night. During the day, we'd go rock climbing or hiking, and I'd take photos with my camera. Those memories of my youth are really precious, but the past few years, I haven't had the time to go camping with my father at all! Every time I talk to him, he tells me he misses our outings. I've got to find time soon to go camping with him, even if it's only for a weekend. I'm sure we'll both have a great time!

Key Words

- [ ] rough it：不自由な生活をする
- [ ] outdoors：戸外で
- [ ] lately：最近
- [ ] meant：mean（意味する）の過去形
- [ ] intensive：集中的な
- [ ] live off the land：自然の恵みで裕福に暮らす
- [ ] youth：青春時代
- [ ] precious：貴重な
- [ ] every time SV ～：～するたびに
- [ ] miss ～：～が（い）なくて寂しい
- [ ] outing：遠出
- [ ] have a great time：最高に楽しい時間を過ごす

Translation

不自由な生活がいいと思ったことは一度もないけど、それでも野外で時間を過ごすことは楽しい。最近は時間がないけど、高校生の頃は、毎年夏になると父とキャンプに行ったなあ。父はかなりたくましい人で、僕にもたくましくなってほしがっていた。だから、夏の間は集中トレーニングしていたんだ。父はキャンプをしに僕を山に連れて行き、1週間過ごしたものだった。近くの川で釣りをしたり、夜はたき火で料理をしたりしながら、自然の恵みで生活したものだった。昼間は、ロッククライミングやハイキングに行って、写真を撮った。そういう青春時代の思い出はとても貴重なものだけど、ここ数年は父とキャンプに行く時間がないんだ。彼と話をするたびに、遠出ができなくて寂しいと言っている。たとえ週末だけでもいいから、彼とキャンプに行く時間を見つけようと思った。2人とも最高の時間を楽しめるに違いないしね！

Point

☐ My dad's a pretty strong guy, and he wanted me to grow up to be strong too.
父はかなりたくましい人で、僕にもたくましく育ってほしがっていた。
* grow up to be ～ 〔成長して～になる〕

↓

★ His daughter grew up to be a cabin attendant.
彼の娘は成長してキャビンアテンダントになった。

Other Expressions

❶ テントを張るのを手伝おうか？
Do you need any help pitching the tent?

❷ 糸に食いついたら、魚をたぐり寄せて。
Once you get a bite on your line, reel the fish in.

❸ そのベリーを摘んだらだめ、毒があるかもしれないから！
Don't pick those berries, they might be poisonous!

❹ 狐色になるまでマシュマロを火にあぶって。
Cook the marshmallows over the fire until they've browned.

❺ バードウォッチングはアウトドア派の人に人気のある余暇。
Bird watching is a popular pastime for outdoorsmen.

❻ 森で熊の足跡を見つけた。
I spotted some bear tracks in the woods.

❼ 私たちは皆、自然と調和して生活できればいいのになあ。
I wish we could all live in harmony with nature.

❽ 息子には強く育ってほしいから、キャンプに行った時は木を切らせるの。
I want my son to grow up strong, so I make him chop wood when we go camping.

❾ ロッククライミングに行く時は、いつもパートナーを連れて行きなさい。
When you go rock climbing, always bring along a partner.

❿ イノシシを見た時、一目散に逃げた！
When I saw a wild boar, I ran off like a speeding bullet!

34 ビーチで

I should pick out a cute swimsuit for the beach.

ビーチ用に可愛い水着を選ばなくちゃ。

One of my co-workers invited me to go to the beach tomorrow. He's kind of cute, so I said 'yes.' I actually started blushing when I realized he was asking me out! I've only spoken to him once or twice, but he and I have a lot in common. I ran into him in the lunch room, and he kept talking about his exercise regimen. I mentioned my own gym routine, and we really hit it off. I should pick out a cute swimsuit for the beach. Since it's the first time he and I will be hanging out outside of work, I shouldn't go with something daring. I'll wear a modest one-piece swimsuit. I also need to stop by the department store and pick up some sunblock. I have fair skin, so I burn quite easily. I'll need to get SPF 30 sunblock at the very least! I wonder if I should make some snacks for us tomorrow. Maybe I can impress him with my home cooking! I'll make something healthy that both of us can enjoy!

Key Words

- invite：求める、依頼する
- blush：赤面する
- realize：気づく
- ask out ～：～をデートに誘う
- in common：共通した
- regimen：メニュー
- mention：言及する
- routine：日課
- hang out：付き合う
- daring：大胆な
- modest：控えめな
- fair skin：色白の肌
- snack：軽食
- impress：印象付ける

Translation

同僚の一人から明日、ビーチに行かないかって誘われたの。彼は、まあまあ魅力的な人だから「うん」と言ったわ。実を言うと、誘っているんだって気づいた時、私は赤面しちゃった。1回か2回しか彼とは話したことがなかったんだけど、共通点はたくさんあるの。食堂で偶然彼に会った時、彼は自分のエクササイズメニューのことをずっと話していたわ。私が日課にしている自分の運動のことを話したら意気投合しちゃったの。ビーチ用に可愛い水着を選ばなくちゃ。会社の外でのお付き合いは初めてになるから、大胆な水着はやめておこう。控えめなワンピースの水着を着ようかな。デパートに寄ってサンブロックも買わなくちゃ。肌が白いから日焼けしやすいの。ともかく、ＳＰＦ30のサンブロックは買わなくちゃ。明日の軽食を作った方がいいかなあ。きっと、家庭料理で彼に印象づけることができるわ。2人とも楽しめるような健康食を作ろう！

Point

☐ He's kind of cute, so I said 'yes.'
彼はまあまあ魅力的な人だから「うん」と言ったわ。
＊ kind of 〜 〔まあまあ〜〕的確な表現が見つからない時や、曖昧にぼかす時の表現。sort of 〜も同じように使う。

↓

★ I kind of like this song.
この歌はまぁまぁ気に入っている。

Other Expressions

❶ ひなたぼっこをするのが大好きだからビーチに行くの！
I go to the beach because I love having fun in the sun!

❷ ビーチサイドのレストランはお高くとまってないから、カジュアルな物を選んで、ジーンズとTシャツを着ていくわ。
The beachside restaurant is not fancy. I'll go with something casual and wear jeans and a T-shirt.

❸ ヨーロッパではひものビキニが流行っていると聞いたけど、そんなの私には絶対着られないわ！
I heard thong bikinis are popular in Europe. I could never wear those!

❹ 1日中ビーチでぶらぶらしてたから、日焼けがひどい。
I hung out at the beach all day, and now I've got terrible sunburn.

❺ 日焼け止めを塗らなかったから、彼の皮膚は真っ赤だった。
His skin was red as a lobster because he didn't wear sunblock.

❻ 健康的な小麦色の女性が好き。
I like girls with a healthy tan.

❼ 色白の肌なら、ちゃんと小麦色にはならないわ。
If you're fair-skinned, you can't tan properly.

❽ 波が強すぎて飲まれそうになった！
The waves were so strong they almost pulled me under!

❾ シュノーケルを持ってきた。
I brought my snorkeling gear along with me.

❿ 週末のビーチにはいつも人の群れ。
There's always a mob of people at the beach during the weekend.

35 化粧

They end up looking like clowns.

彼らはピエロのように見えてしまうわ。

Using cosmetics is a fact of life for a working woman. Every morning before I head to work, I spend about fifteen minutes in front of the bathroom mirror making my face. I honestly find it a bit rude when I see the young ladies trying to put on makeup on the train or in the car. Aren't they embarrassed at all by how they look? I'm sure many young women today have hectic schedules, but they should at least make the effort to put on their makeup before they leave the house! What's worse, they often cake on too much makeup, so they end up looking like clowns. As for myself, I only put on a bit of lip gloss, some concealer to hide blemishes, and some eye shadow. Working at an office is one thing; being at a party is another, so you don't need to wear that much makeup, after all!

Key Words

- cosmetics：化粧品
- fact of life：避けられない現実
- honestly：正直に言って
- put on makeup：化粧する
- embarrassed：恥ずかしい
- hectic：てんやわんやの
- make the effort：努力する
- cake：厚く塗る
- clown：ピエロ
- as for 〜：〜については
- blemish：シミ
- after all：やはり、結局

Translation

化粧品を使うことは働く女性にとっては避けられない現実。出勤する前に毎朝、洗面所の鏡の前で化粧にかける時間は約15分。正直言って、若い女性たちが電車や車の中で化粧しようとしているのを見ると、ちょっと無作法な感じがするわ。どう見られているか全然恥ずかしくないのかしら？　確かに、てんやわんやのスケジュールの若い女性がたくさんいるけど、少なくとも家を出る前に化粧をする努力をするべきだわ。もっと悪いことに、厚化粧をしている場合もよくあるから、ピエロのように見えてしまうのよね。私が塗るのは、リップグロスとシミ隠しのコンシーラー、それとアイシャドーだけ。会社で働くのとパーティーに参加するのは別のことだから、やっぱりそんなに厚化粧は必要ないわ！

Point

☐ **What's worse, they often cake on too much makeup.**
もっと悪いことに、厚化粧をすることもよくある。
* what's worse〔さらに悪いことに〕= to make matters worse

⬇

★ **It was getting colder. What's worse, it began to snow.**
だんだん寒くなってきたが、さらに悪いことに雪が降り出した。

Other Expressions

❶ ちょっとアイライナーつけすぎじゃない。ピエロみたいだよ！
You're wearing way too much eyeliner. You look like a clown!

❷ リップスティックつけすぎないようにね。こすれて汚くなるよ。
Be careful you don't apply too much lipstick. It will smear.

❸ このスキンクリームは最高！　肌がずっときれいになる。
This skin cream is great! It helps keep my skin clear.

❹ 化粧品カウンターのあの女性、試供品を配っている！
The lady at the cosmetics counter is giving out free samples!

❺ 頬紅をつけると頬の色が引き立つ。
Wearing blush brings out the color in my cheeks.

❻ マスカラの色合いがあなたに似合わない。
That shade of mascara doesn't become you.

❼ ホントに黄緑のマニキュア液をつけようと思ってるの？
Are you really going to wear bright green nail polish?

❽ 彼女は化粧直しにトイレに行った。
She went to the restroom to powder her face.

❾ 化粧しすぎると肌荒れの原因になることもある。
Wearing too much makeup can cause your skin to break out.

❿ 肌に吹き出物が出ちゃった。ファンデーションアレルギーかなあ。
My skin broke out in a rash. I think I'm allergic to this foundation.

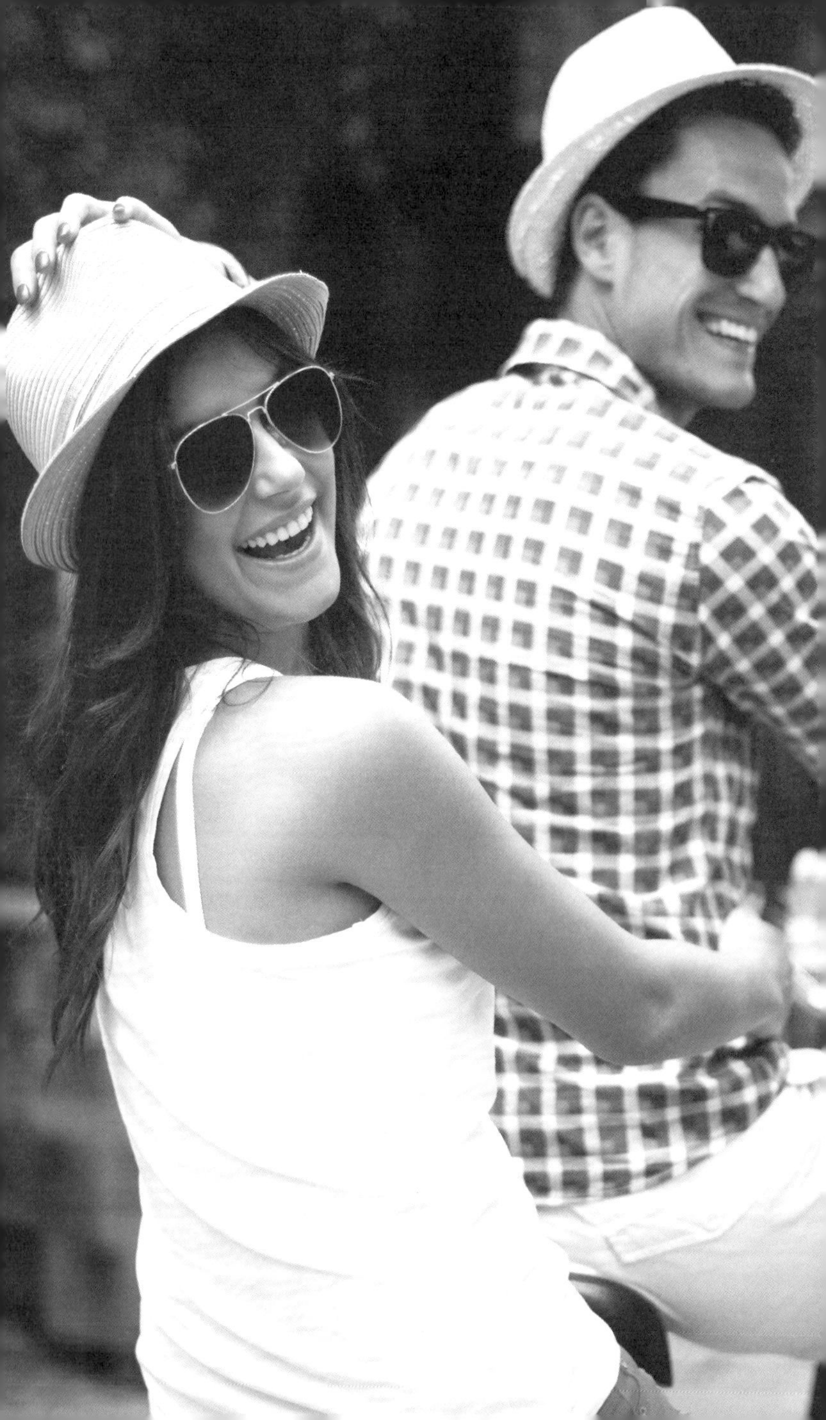

Just trust yourself,
then you will know how to live.
- Goethe

自分を信じるだけでいい。
そうしたら、生きる道が見えてくるから。
ゲーテ

36 ボランティア

I've joined a volunteer group in my community.
地域のボランティア団体に入ったんだ。

I'm dead tired! I spent the whole day picking up litter near the elementary school. If you're wondering why I spent the day picking up trash, the reason is that I've joined a volunteer group in my community. As to why I joined a volunteer group, I suppose you could say it was out of a need to socialize with other people. Well, the truth is that the volunteer group is mostly made up of women around my age, so I suppose I have ulterior motives. That is to say, I'm looking for a girlfriend, and there seem to be a lot of eligible ladies in the group. But does the reason really matter? In the end, I'm making a difference in the community by helping clean up the neighborhood, assisting at senior centers, and collecting food for food drives. So what if I'm also trying to score a few dates? It's totally normal for a young guy like me!

Key Words

- [ ] dead：完全に
- [ ] litter：ゴミ
- [ ] elementary school：小学校
- [ ] trash：ゴミ
- [ ] as to 〜：〜に関して
- [ ] socialize with 〜：〜と交流する
- [ ] be made up of 〜：〜で構成される
- [ ] ulterior motive：下心（隠された動機）
- [ ] that is to say：すなわち、つまり
- [ ] eligible：適確な、相応しい
- [ ] matter：重要である
- [ ] make a difference：役に立つ（本来は「違いを生じる」）
- [ ] senior center：高齢者センター
- [ ] food drive：困窮者に食事を提供する慈善事業
- [ ] score a date：デートの約束をうまく取りつける

Translation

もうくたくた。小学校の近くで丸1日かけてゴミ拾い。何で1日かけてゴミ拾いなの？ と思っているとしたら、その理由は、地域のボランティア団体に入ったからなんだ。何でボランティア団体に入ったのかについては、他の人たちとの交流を図る必要性からだと言っていいかな。そうだなあ、実は、そのボランティア団体は、主に僕と同年代の女性で構成されているから、下心からかもね。つまり、僕はガールフレンドを探しているんだけど、その団体には相応しい女性がたくさんいそうってこと。でも実際、理由って大事なことかなぁ？ 結局は、近所を清掃したり、高齢者センターでお手伝いしたり、慈善事業のために食料を集めたりして、地域社会に役に立っている。だから、デートの約束をいくつか取り付けようとしたっていいんじゃない？ 僕みたいな若い男にとっては、至極普通のことだと思う。

Point

☐ **What if I'm also trying to score a few dates?**
デートの約束をいくつか取り付けようとしたっていいんじゃない？
＊ What if SV 〜？ {〜したらどうなるの→〜してもかまうものか}

⬇

★ **What if I fail?**
失敗したってかまうものか。

Other Expressions

❶ 毎週金曜日の夜は老人ホームでボランティア。

I volunteer at the old folks' home every Friday night.

❷ ボランティアで彼は共同体意識を発揮した。

By volunteering, he showed he had community spirit.

❸ 高校のボランティア部は5人の若い学生からなっていた。

The high school's volunteer club was composed of five young students.

❹ 地元の路上生活者用の施設に寄付するために古着を集めている。

I'm collecting old clothes to donate at the local homeless shelter.

❺ 赤十字の献血運動で多くの大学生が献血をした。

Many college students gave blood at the blood drive for the Red Cross.

❻ チャリティーボックスに余った小銭を入れませんか？

Why don't you drop your spare change in that charity box?

❼ 彼はチャリティーに収入の10%を寄付している。

He gives 10 percent of his income to charity.

❽ アメリカのクリスマスは恵まれない人たちを助ける時。

In America, Christmas is the time to help the less fortunate.

❾ 公園のゴミ拾いを手伝ってくれない？

Could you help picking up litter at the park?

❿ 人助けをしたってわかると心がホント温まる。

Knowing that I've helped people really warms my heart.

37 女子会で

Yesterday, I had a girls' night out.

昨日、女子会だったの。

Yesterday, my female college friends and I had a girls' night out. We do this about once a month, as it gives us a chance to catch up on our lives and to chitchat and trade stories about our old classmates. My friends are always making fun of me for being unlucky in love. They tease me about how I'm going to end up an old maid. It's hard to disagree with them, considering my luck so far. They've even offered to fix me up on dates, but I keep begging off. Most of my college friends have boyfriends or are engaged to be married, though they're constantly complaining about them. Besides gossiping and joking around, we also usually drink a bit and go karaoke. Some of my friends are pretty good amateur singers! We always sing the latest J-Pop songs, as well as some older songs from our college days.

Key Words

- girls' night out：女子だけで行く夜のお出かけ
- catch up on 〜：遅れを取り戻す
- chitchat：うわさ話をする
- trade：交換する
- make fun of 〜：〜をからかう
- be unlucky in love：失恋する
- tease：からかう
- old maid：オールドミス
- fix up：手配する、仲を取り持つ
- beg off：丁重に断る
- constantly：常に
- joke around：馬鹿な振る舞いをする

Translation

昨日は大学時代の友だちと女子会だったの。生活の遅れを取り戻し、昔のクラスメートのうわさ話や情報交換をする機会になるから、ひと月に1回くらいはこうしているの。友だちは私が失恋したことをいつもからかってばかり。オールドミスになっちゃうよって私をからかうの。今までのめぐり合わせを考えると、彼女たちに反論することは難しい。デートの約束を取り持ってくれるとまで言ってくれるんだけど、断りっぱなし。大学時代の友だちはほとんどボーイフレンドがいたり、婚約をしたりしているの。いつも相手の不満ばかり言っているけどね。うわさ話や馬鹿なことをしているだけじゃなく、普段はお酒も少し飲んでカラオケもするわ。友だちの中にはかなり上手なアマチュア歌手もいるの。大学時代の古い歌だけじゃなく最新のJポップの歌も、いつも歌っているのよ。

Point

☐ It's hard to disagree with them, considering my luck so far.
今までのめぐり合わせを考えると、彼女たちに反論することが難しい。
* considering 〜 〔〜を考えると、〜の割には〕

↓

★ My mother looks pretty young, considering her age.
母は歳の割にはかなり若く見える。

Other Expressions

❶ 夫はひと月に1回男の夜の会に行く。
My husband has a boys' night out once a month.

❷ 女の子の友だちと集まって有名人のうわさ話を交換するのが大好き。
I love getting together with my girlfriends and sharing celebrity gossip.

❸ 地元のパブに行って、ビールを何杯か飲もう。
Let's hit the local pub and grab a couple of beers.

❹ 僕の彼女は女友だちとクラブに行って踊って飲むのが大好き。
My girlfriend loves to go clubbing with her gal pals.

❺ 友だちは彼女を誘ったけど、彼女は今晩は家にいることに決めた。
Her friends invited her out, but she decided to stay in tonight.

❻ 夕べは夜更かししちゃったから寝坊した。
I overslept because I stayed out too late last night.

❼ 今週の土曜日の夜は女友だちと集まることになってるの。だから男子は参加不可！
I'm having a get-together with all my female friends this Saturday night. No boys allowed!

❽ 彼女は女友だちといる時だけ自分らしくなれる。
She can only be herself around her female friends.

❾ 飲み過ぎちゃったからふらふら。
I feel tipsy because I had too much to drink.

❿ 彼女はシャイだからビールを2・3本体に入れないとカラオケができない。
She's too shy to sing karaoke without a couple of beers in her.

38 結婚観

We decided on a division of duties at home.

家庭での役割分担を決めた。

Since we're going to be married soon, I think it's time Karen and I decided on a division of duties at home. I'm not an old-fashioned sort of guy. Since Karen and I are both going to be working full-time, I think we should divide the housework equally. Each of us should do housework according to our skills. I'm a terrible cook, so I'll leave the cooking to Karen. I can wash the dishes, take out the trash, and help with cleaning our apartment. Karen can do the laundry, wash the windows, and do the grocery shopping. I thought this was a good plan, but Karen disagrees! It turns out that she wants to do all the housework as well as work full-time. I think this is a ridiculous idea. She says that she does all the housework as a single woman, so why shouldn't she do it after she's married? I told her that it would be unfair to make her do everything, but she wouldn't hear of it. She's quite a stubborn woman, but that's one of the reasons I love her.

Key Words

- decide on 〜：〜に決める
- division：分担
- duties：役割
- sort：種類
- housework：家事
- equally：平等に
- according to 〜：〜に従って
- leave A to B：AをBに任せる
- laundry：洗濯
- It turns out that SV 〜：結局〜だとわかる
- ridiculous：馬鹿げた
- unfair：不公平な
- quite：全く
- stubborn：頑固な

Translation

もうすぐ結婚するから、カレンと僕は家庭での役割分担を決める頃だと思う。僕は古くさい種類の男じゃない。カレンも僕もフルタイムで働くつもりだから、家事を平等に分担した方がいいと思う。僕たちはそれぞれの技量に従って家事をするべきだよ。僕は料理がへたくそだから料理はカレンに任せよう。皿洗いとゴミ出しとアパートの掃除の手伝いは僕ができる。カレンは洗濯と窓拭きと食料品の買い物ができる。これは良いプランだと思っていたんだけど、カレンは反対しているんだ。結局、彼女はフルタイムで働くだけじゃなくて家事も全部やりたがっている。これって馬鹿げた考えだと思うなあ。独身女性として今は家事を全部しているって彼女は言っているんだから、結婚後はそうすべきじゃない。全部彼女にやらせるのは不公平だと彼女に言ったけど、どうしても聞こうともしなかった。彼女は全くの頑固もの。だけどそれも僕が彼女を愛している理由のひとつなんだ。

Point

☐ **I think it's time Karen and I decided on a division of duties at home.**

カレンと僕は家庭での役割分担を決める頃だと思う。

 ＊ It's time S ＋過去形の動詞 {もう〜する時間だ} time の前に about を入れれば、「そろそろ」、high を入れれば「もうとっくに」の意味が強調される。

↓

★ **It's time I went to bed.**

もう寝る時間だ。

Other Expressions

❶ 新婚夫婦は最近、マンションを購入。
The newlyweds recently bought an apartment.

❷ 来週の日曜日に彼らは結婚25周年を祝う。
They will celebrate their 25th wedding anniversary next Sunday.

❸ 彼らの3人の子供たちは記念日の祝いのお金を出してくれる。
Their three children will pay for the anniversary celebration.

❹ 家事の中で一番簡単なのは洗濯。
One of the easiest household chores is doing the laundry.

❺ 食器洗い器を買ったから皿洗いは朝飯前。
Since I bought a dishwasher, doing the dishes is a snap.

❻ アイロンがけは一番大変な家事のひとつということがわかったわ。
I find that ironing is one of the hardest household chores.

❼ 新しいコーヒーメーカーならコーヒーを淹れるのが簡単。
My new coffee machine makes it easy to brew coffee.

❽ テレビの前に座りながら洗濯物をたたむの。
I fold the laundry while sitting in front of the TV.

❾ 土曜の夜は、よく夕食に何組かの夫婦を招待するの。
We often invite other couples for supper on Saturday night.

❿ 私が帰宅すると妻はいつも温かい食事を用意していてくれる。
My wife always has a hot meal waiting for me when I get home.

Profile

清水 建二　*Kenji Shimizu*

東京都浅草生まれ。上智大学文学部英文学科を卒業後、大手予備校講師、ガイド通訳士、進学の名門・埼玉県立浦和高等学校などを経て、現在は埼玉県立川口高等学校教諭。基礎から上級まで、わかりやすくユニークな教え方には定評がある。著書は、『世界一速く英語脳に変わる本』『48パターンだけですぐに話せる！　英語ペラペラブック』『たった1500語ですぐに通じる　グロービッシュ英単語』（すべて総合法令出版）、シリーズ累計26万部突破の『パターンで話せる　英会話1秒レッスン』（成美文庫）、ベストセラー『新編集　語源とイラストで一気に覚える英単語』（成美堂出版）、『連想式にみるみる身につく　語源で英単語』（学研教育出版）など、60冊以上。『似ている英単語使い分けBOOK』（ベレ出版）は台湾、香港、韓国で翻訳出版され、語学書のロングセラーとなっている。

ホセ・バラガン・ボスエル　*Jose E. Barragan Bothwell*

プエルトリコ大学にて、ジャーナリズムと文学の学士を取得。同大学院にて英米文学の修士課程を修了。
2005年に来日し、埼玉の公立高校や私立の高校などで教鞭を執ったのち、2013年に帰国。現在はプエルトリコ大学英語講師。趣味はスペイン旅行や日本映画の鑑賞。

「私」を語れば、英語は話せる。

2015年 9月 5日 初版発行

著者	清水 建二
	ホセ・バラガン・ボスエル
ブックデザイン	土屋 和泉
発行者	野村 直克
発行所	総合法令出版株式会社
	〒103-0001
	東京都中央区日本橋小伝馬町 15-18
	ユニゾ小伝馬町ビル 9 階
	電話　03-5623-5121
印刷・製本	中央精版印刷株式会社
音声制作協力	キャプラン株式会社Jプレゼンスアカデミー
音声ナレーション	アラミンタ・ハモンド
	ジェフ・ハッシュ

視覚障害その他の理由で活字のままではこの本を利用出来ない人のために、営利を目的とする場合を除き「録音図書」「点字図書」「拡大図書」等の製作をすることを認めます。その際は著作権者、または、出版社までご連絡ください。

©Kenji Shimizu/Jose E. Barragan Bothwell 2015 Printed in Japan
ISBN978-4-86280-464-8
落丁・乱丁本はお取替えいたします。
総合法令出版ホームページ　http://www.horei.com/

本書の表紙、写真、イラスト、本文はすべて著作権法で保護されています。
著作権法で定められた例外を除き、これらを許諾なしに複写、コピー、印刷物やインターネットのWebサイト、メール等に転載することは違法となります。

清水建二氏の好評既刊

世界一速く
英語脳に変わる本

清水建二著　ウィリアム・J・カリー監修

定価：1800円+税 ｜ 四六判 ｜ 208ページ

ISBN 978-4-86280-226-2

中学レベルの簡単な英文パターンをたくさん読んで聴くだけで、英語がどんどん話せるようになる！英語を習得するには、難しい英文や長文からマスターしようとしても逆効果。「秒速パターン練習」と「倍速リスニング」によって、表現力と会話力が短期間で身に付く。英語脳を鍛えるCD2枚付き。

48パターンだけですぐに話せる！
英語ペラペラブック

清水建二著　ウィリアム・J・カリー監修

定価：1800円+税 ｜ 四六判 ｜ 224ページ

ISBN 978-4-86280-261-3

日常の様々なシーンに対応した48パターンの使えるフレーズを使いこなせば、英語が口から溢れだす！　英語脳にて、「言いたいことが素早く英語に変換できない」を解消！「会話を盛り上げる」フレーズも収録。これで、ネイティブともスムーズに話せる！　CD2枚付き。

たった1500語ですぐに通じる
グロービッシュ英単語

清水建二著　ウィリアム・J・カリー監修

定価：1000円+税 ｜ 新書 ｜ 272ページ

ISBN 978-4-86280-271-2

日本企業の海外移転や海外企業との統合が進み、ますます「英語熱」が高まっている。そんな折に登場したのが「グロービッシュ」。
単語はたった1500語だけ、複雑な発音は気にしない、熟語や比喩を使わない等、シンプルなルールに基づいた、「非ネイティブ」のための新しい英語術グロービッシュで使われる1500の英単語を、この1冊にすべて凝縮した、中学レベルのシンプルな英文で覚える、グロービッシュ英単語帳。全文、無料音声ダウンロード付き。